Seminal Sociological Writings: From Auguste Comte to Max Weber

Seminal Sociological Writings:
From Auguste Comte to Max Weber

An Anthology of Groundbreaking Works that Created the Science of Sociology

Gordian Knot Books

An Imprint of Richard Altschuler & Associates, Inc.

New York

Seminal Sociological Writings: From Auguste Comte to Max Weber: An Anthology of Groundbreaking Works that Created the Science of Sociology. For information contact the publisher at 100 W. 57th Street, NY, NY 10019, 212- 397-7233, or RAltschuler@rcn.com.

Library of Congress Control Number: 2010920942
CIP data for this book are available from the Library of Congress

ISBN-13: 978-1-884092-97-8

Cover Design and Layout: Josh Garfield

Printed in the United States of America

DEDICATION

This book is dedicated to social scientists everywhere
who have a unique vision and the courage to express it

TABLE OF CONTENTS

Foreword

Sociology is an academic discipline that has become increasingly well known to the general public. But some of the best known books in sociology have not necessarily been the best books in sociology. Also, there is much extremely valuable writing buried in refereed journals and somewhat technical academic collections. A young scholar approaching the history of writing in the general area of social sciences knows a few key writers in psychology and economics, but often it is not as clear which authors represent sociology. This edited volume will provide an excellent introduction to some of the work of many of the leading classical contributors.

The sixteen sociologists represented in this edited collection provide an overview of the historical development of the discipline of sociology between Auguste Comte (1798-1857) and Max Weber (1864-1920), a period of about one hundred years (*circa* 1820-1920). Each author is certainly worth getting to know. Students who major in sociology often hear the names but do not begin to actually read the work. The importance of reading the original work of classical contributors cannot be overemphasized. If we learn about a thinker second-hand from a general survey textbook, then we will not have the same depth of knowledge as we can gain from reading the author's original words. Of course, the correct interpretation of a text always requires knowing something about the political, economic, cultural and military context. The intellectual *Zeitgeist* must be familiar enough for the student to have some idea why a particular topic may be of interest. It is partially for that reason that textbooks on classical theory will always remain important. But after the student has acquired some foundation in history and philosophy, then it is possible to begin to read the classical writers. For many students with an intellectual bent, these writers will become more than just names.

Learning about classical theory has been an important part of my own intellectual biography. It has been my quest to try to grasp the history of sociological thought. Ever since reading Lewis Coser's magnificent textbook (1977), the whole idea of sociological theory has really come alive for me. The thinkers represented in this book are not just dry-as-dust old-timers with nothing relevant to say to a new generation. Quite the opposite. They tackled many of the same problems that confront everyone, young and old, at the beginning of the second decade of the twenty-first century. Those include problems related to liberal versus conservative political principles as they pertain to the notion of "legitimate authority." When is a social collectivity well organized? How reasonable is it to consider contemporary global "Neo-liberalism" to be an outgrowth of conservative Utilitarianism?

Despite the fact that they could be conceived of as quite different, there is almost complete unanimity among professional, academic sociologists that the three classical authors everyone should know at least a bit about are Marx, Durkheim, and Weber. Marx was born first (1818-1883), but he is not the first major thinker accepted into the canon. Due to his political activism and the critical nature of his work, Karl Marx was not initially recognized as a sociologist or a founder of social science. He was often considered a Marxist rather than a sociologist, particularly by those who were convinced of the scientific merits of his critique of bourgeois science. His work on the political economy of modern capitalist societies was thought of by many as "scientific Communism" and hence not sociology. But after WWII, there was a renewed interest in the sociological component of Marx's work. Albert Salomon stressed the notion that sociological theorists were always debating with Marx's ghost. The "ghost" metaphor works because in many cases there was very little explicit mention of Marx or Marxism. The confrontation with Marx often had to be read between the lines (Zeitlin 2001: 194-196). Weber's relationship to Marx's theory is somewhat clouded by the fact that many of the things which Weber said about Marxism were comments made in the heat of political upheaval following WWI. Weber did not write a long monograph about Marx's theory of capital. Instead, he continued to work on problems of comparative economic history. His dissertation on early Medieval trade is filled with implicit assumptions probably borrowed from Marx and other economic historians. While many textbooks make Marx and Weber representatives of quite different and opposed viewpoints, it may be more heuristic to see Weber as continuing Marx's work, but expanding it to cover not only economic class but also political power and cultural status (Zeitlin 2006: 194-258).

The third member of the trinity is Durkheim. Durkheim is sometimes caricatured as simply a Positivist, but there is more to Durkheim than his book on *Suicide* or his *Rules of Sociological Method*. Durkheim is not a strict Positivist and Utilitarian and is, in fact, incisive in his critique of extreme forms of scientism and laissez faire (Parsons 1949: 343-375). Some commentators have stressed the importance for his mature theory of *The Elementary Forms of Religious Life*. When before WWII Talcott Parsons attempted to convince his American audience that both Weber and Durkheim are important for the discipline of sociology, he had little trouble with the mention of Durkheim's name. But he did have some difficulty moving beyond the stereotyped version of Durkheim. In order to see the similarities between Durkheim and Weber, it is important to compare the whole life's work of the one with the other. Weber's oeuvre and Durkheim's oeuvre are both abundant, and there is lots of room for finding similarities in their sociological approach to social life. Not the least important of the links between Durkheim and Weber is the stress on religion and religious organization (Parsons 1949: 409-450, 579-639). Today we sometimes refer to the approach common to Weber and the later Durkheim as "Interpretive." Interpretive sociology contributes to the understanding of human beings as agents engaged in meaningful symbolic interaction on the basis of shared "significant symbols." Weber and Durkheim both did excellent Interpretive work and indeed Weber designated his approach as "interpretive sociology" (*verstehende Soziologie*). The understanding of human cultural values and meaning systems is also important to the young and the very old Karl Marx. One way to think of Marx's *Capital* is to see it as only a small part of the total oeuvre that he would have liked to have completed. The "Outline" (*Grundrisse*) that Marx wrote before he completed *Capital* Volume I gives an indication of the breadth of Marx's sociological interests. The Frankfurt School of Critical Theory proposes a "Critical Theory" version of sociology that has many echoes of the Interpretive work of Weber and Durkheim.

Other authors on almost everyone's list of seminal thinkers are Mead, Simmel, and Veblen. This is not the place to review them individually, but a brief mention is warranted. George Herbert Mead is very important for "Social Behaviorism" as a critique of Positivistic-Scientistic Behaviorism, and Mead is now viewed as the philosophical source of Symbolic Interactionism. Simmel was also a wide-ranging social philosopher and sociological theorist whose work on the dyad versus the triad, social types like the flirt and the miser, Rembrandt, the philosophy of money, and the underlying foundations for sociology as a special science deserves to be well known. Thorstein Veblen's iconoclastic critique of American class privilege and the way in which the "leisure class" manipulates social status through "conspicuous consumption" is just as radical now as when he wrote it. Some students have a bit of difficulty reading Veblen, but once his Norwegian-American cadence is understood, he becomes every bit as interesting as contemporary public intellectuals like Noam Chomsky.

Not always as frequently emphasized, but powerful thinkers in their own right, are Cooley, Giddings, Le Bon, Sumner, Tarde, Thomas, Tönnies and Ward. Lester Ward, for example, was a tireless field worker and applied many of the latest scientific techniques to the detailed study of empirical problems. Ferdinand Tönnies' famous theory of *Gemeinschaft* and *Gesellschaft* has had a great deal of impact on rural sociology but his critique of Marx is not as well known.

Of course, even this group of sixteen outstanding contributors to classical theory only scratches the surface. But anyone who reads this book carefully will have an excellent basis for fully understanding many of the contemporary debates concerning micro and macro issues, agency versus structure, functions versus exploitation, primary groups, dyads, symbolic interaction, crowds, masses, and the general nature of modern and postmodern capitalism.

The selections in this collection are partially American and partially European. This collection favors American thinkers and has eight thinkers who originally wrote in English. The only Englishman represented in this collection is Spencer. The Americans are strongly represented through work by Cooley, Giddings, Mead, Sumner, Thomas, Veblen and Ward. The remaining eight authors are all continental Europeans. The French thinkers are Comte, Durkheim, Le Bon and Tarde. The German thinkers are Marx, Simmel, Tönnies and Weber. There are no Russian, Polish, Dutch or Italian European thinkers emphasized in this reader, yet there are dozens of authors who could have been considered (Timasheff 1967: 45-57, 90-98, 122-127).[1]

Another way to think about the writers is in terms of their similarities and differences. One of the most important schools of thought (or, Meta-Paradigms) of classical theory, is the Positivist Paradigm. When Comte published his first important work in the 1820s he set the foundation for at least one major European stream of academic work that quickly had influence outside of France. Comte invented the French word *sociologie*, an amalgam of a Latin and a Greek word. He had wanted to call the new discipline social physics, but he had been preceded by Adolph Quetelet, a French-speaking Belgian astronomer and statistician. So Comte coined a new word and that neologism has stuck. It is now used in ways that go far beyond what Comte initially envisaged as the new Positive science. It is entirely fitting that the first selection is from Comte's truly seminal *Positive Philosophy*.

Comte's French word *sociologie* was quickly adopted by Herbert Spencer (1820-1903), and it is to Spencer that we primarily owe the adoption of the term in English. Spencer, in turn, influenced William Graham Sumner. Their Positivist and Functionalist orientation has been challenged by a number of the other authors. For example, in France Le Bon and Tarde took different approaches to the Comte-Durkheim Positivist School. In America Lester Ward was an opponent of Spencer and Sumner's laissez faire ideas.

This first volume contains the work of important thinkers. Almost every sociologist recognizes the sixteen individuals as contributors to the discipline. However, the collection is not complete and a second volume may provide a selection that will help to round out the picture by including women, African-Americans (e.g., W. E. B. DuBois), and writers from other nationalities like India, China, Korea and Japan. Yet, the fact that others could have been included should not make anyone assume that those thinkers represented in this collection do not belong here.

The title is "seminal sociological writings" and the "groundbreaking works" assembled here do not all have to be contributions to sociological theory per se. But it is reasonable to argue that all the authors can legitimately be considered theorists. All of them wrote from a broad perspective, based on wide reading and philosophical insight. Many of these theorists also travelled extensively, particularly within Europe or America. (Some, like Weber, did venture from America to Europe, and many, like Mead, studied in Germany.) These selections contain the classical "sociological imagination" and are not the product of overly abstract "grand theory" or mere "abstract empiricism" (Mills 1959). Most can be considered representative of what Robert K. Merton (1957: 280) had in mind when he discussed "Middle Range Theory."[2]

We do have to be somewhat careful when we discuss classical *sociological theorists*. Many people have made important contributions to the discipline who may not necessarily have done a great deal of theorizing. For example, Dorothy Swaine Thomas, the wife of W. I. Thomas, jointly helped to formulate the famous statement of the "Definition of the Situation" (Bakker 2009). They co-authored *The Child in America* (1928). But even though she became a President of the ASA, Dorothy Thomas was not given much recognition as a theorist. That may in part be due to the gender norms of the 1930s and 1940s. But she mostly made her mark in applied demography and population research, and so, despite recent comments (Smith 1995), she may not have been an important "theorist" per se. In adding women to the list it is important to focus on those who truly contributed to theory, and surely Harriet Martineau, Florence Nightingale, Marianne Weber and Jane Addams belong to that list.

Nevertheless, it is very important to read the works of these sixteen men. They are not merely "dead white males." They are important intellectuals who provided a significant set of ideas. Those ideas constitute the "idea units" that have been relevant to many branches of sociology since the early part of the twentieth century. As we move through the second decade of the twenty-first century, we can easily see the year 2020 on the horizon. This work introduces those interested in sociology to authors and concepts that will still be important at that time.

J. I. (Hans) Bakker, Ph.D.
University of Guelph

References:

Bakker, J. I. (Hans). 2009. "The Definition of the Situation." *Blackwell Encyclopedia of Sociology,* (ed.) Ritzer, George. Malden, MA: Blackwell Publishers.

Coser, Lewis A. 1977 [1971]. *Masters of Sociological Thought: Ideas in Historical and Social Context. Second Edition.* New York: Harcourt, Brace, Jovanovich.

Merton, Robert K. 1957 [1949]. *Social Theory and Social Structure. Revised and Enlarged Edition.* New York: Free Press.

Mills, C. Wright. 1959. *The Sociological Imagination.* New York: Oxford.

Parsons, Talcott. 1949 [1937]. *The Structure of Social Action: A Study in Social Theory with Special Reference to a Group of Recent European Writers.* Glencoe, Illinois: The Free Press. [Originally published by McGraw-Hill.]

Smith, R. S. 1995. "Giving Credit Where Credit is Due: Dorothy Swaine Thomas and the 'Thomas Theorem'." *The American Sociologist* 26 (4): 9-28.

Timasheff, Nicholas S. 1967 [1955]. *Sociological Theory: Its Nature and Growth.* New York: Random House.

[1]Timasheff (1967) is the first textbook on sociological theory that I ever read. It left a lasting impression. However, it suffers from encyclopedic completeness. It has a bit too much discussion of thinkers like "Gumplowicz and Ratzenhofer" and relies more on Russian thinkers than most non-Russian authors would do.

[2] Merton's example of "reference group theory" as a way of consolidating several empirical formulations of similar phenomena is a reasonable way of intuitively understanding Middle Range Theory, but Merton does not adequately clarify boundaries and precisely what theories of the middle range can and cannot encompass.

Editor's Preface

Out of the ashes and rubble of the French and Industrial Revolutions sociology was born. Its early founders were not formally trained or academically credentialed "sociologists," of course, since the discipline was just emerging. Rather, they were philosophers, mathematicians, physicians, attorneys, clergymen, political activists and others who had at least one thing in common: they passionately wanted to understand the nature of human societies, individual behavior, and social relationships from an objective viewpoint, using methodologies based on the physical sciences, rather than through philosophical speculation or religious belief and faith. Many of them also wanted to decrease the problems in human life, eliminate the causes of suffering altogether, justify social inequalities based on evolutionary principles drawn from biology, or simply understand what makes us "tick," among other powerful motivations for creating and developing a "science of society."

Thus, beginning around the middle of the nineteenth century, a new discipline arose that was different from any before it, with a new perspective about human beings, societies, and cultures. But it didn't emerge fullblown, of course; rather, it was more like a toddler, who has to learn how to crawl before it can walk. So the pioneering sociologists were concerned—preoccupied one might say—with defining their new field and its basic concepts, methods, ideas, and theories. They asked such fundamental questions as "What is sociology?" "How is society possible?" and "What is a social fact?" among a multitude of others. For about ninety years, roughly between 1830 and 1920, the new discipline of sociology was forged, grew, blossomed, and, by around the turn of the twentieth century, the "science of society" had became firmly rooted in college and university departments throughout America and Europe.

The Value of Primary Source Documents

If you are interested in the origins of sociology, then reading books *about* the founders and their seminal works can prove to be a rewarding experience; and the interpreters and explicators of these works have much to offer the interested reader and student of social science and intellectual history in general. Such "second order" information, however, is no substitute for the experience you will have and the depth of understanding you will gain by reading the original works of the founders themselves, which are presented in this anthology. While a few other readers exist that contain some original writings by the early sociologists, this anthology uniquely assembles a rich and varied collection of seminal writings from journals and books by many of the creators of sociology.

These primary source documents will allow you to experience how the groundbreaking thinkers *introduced* the paradigm-changing constructs that both shattered earlier perceptions of reality and dominate how contemporary social scientists think about and study human relationships, institutions, societies, and cultures. In addition to allowing you to "tune in" to the great theorists' thoughts and reasoning processes *directly,* these primary source documents will give you an invaluable research resource, because they were written by the theorists in the first person, as they were undergoing their groundbreaking theoretical insights and discoveries, and while they were recording, reflecting on, witnessing, and living through the phenomena that engaged them as they occurred.

The Founders Included in the Anthology

In considering the theorists and their writings contained in this book, you may wonder, "Are they the most important founders of sociology?" or "Are they the only founders?" In answer to the first question, virtually all sociologists would agree that many of the theorists in this volume—including Auguste Comte, Herbert Spencer, Karl Marx, Émile Durkheim, Georg Simmel, and Max Weber—could not have been left out of a first edition concerned with the founding of sociology.

As regards the second question, most historians of sociology would answer that other theorists not included in this volume would have made worthy candidates for inclusion. Some are discussed in the Foreword by Dr. Bakker, and thus a second volume, at the least, of writings by sociological founders is warranted.

When considering who to include in this first volume, I especially had in mind certain seminal works they wrote that focus on specific concepts, ideas, and theories that every sociologist, I am certain, would agree basically define the discipline of sociology and its primary concerns. Thus, each of the selections in this anthology focuses on a specific question of primary importance to the discipline, including the following:

- What is a science of society and how can we study it objectively? (Comte)

- What are social classes and why are they inherently in a state of conflict? (Marx)
- How can the theory of evolution teach us about the structure, struggles, and survival of human societies? (Spencer)
- What are the functions of folkways and mores and how do they affect social life in all societies? (Sumner)
- What are social facts and how are they different from physical facts and psychological facts? (Durkheim)
- How do our definitions of situations affect our subsequent thoughts, feelings, and behaviors? (Thomas)
- How did large, modern cities grow out of the small, close-knit communities that preceded them? (Tönnies)
- Why is crowd behavior unique and what dangers does it pose for social order? (Le Bon)
- How is society possible? (Simmel)
- Why are the "I" and the "me" the basic components of human consciousness, and what is their relationship to each other? (Mead)
- What is the role of imitation in social life, and what does it explain about human behavior? (Tarde)
- How is our self-conception affected by the way we think others see us? (Cooley)
- What is the relationship between pure and applied sociology, and when should we use the latter to try to improve society? (Ward)
- How is conspicuous consumption different from other types of consumption, and what roles does it play in the lives of individuals, families, and social classes? (Veblen)
- Do we have a species consciousness, or consciousness of kind, and how does it affect our behavior with others? (Giddings)
- Did religion change people's thoughts and behaviors about economic matters and foster the rise of modern capitalism? (Weber)

The first sociologists asked and answered these and related fundamental questions with dazzling displays of imagination, intellectual prowess, vision, curiosity, and, in some instances, empirical data and methodological rigor. Marx, Durkheim, and Weber, for example—the "holy trinity" of sociology and social science in general—studied their subject matter systematically and with great thoroughness, did qualitative analyses of historical documents, and analyzed quantitative data to help arrive at their conclusions.

Presentation of the Chapters, Citations, and Additional References

The body of the book is divided into sixteen chapters, one for each theorist, presented in chronological order by the year of the theorist's birth, beginning with Auguste Comte (1798) and ending with Max Weber (1864). Theorists with the same birth year are arranged in alphabetical order by last name. Before each seminal writing is presented, the reader is provided with basic bibliographic information about the selection, including the source from which it came, date of publication, and page numbers, and a brief essay about the background of the theorist and significance of the writing for the discipline of sociology.

After the last chapter, the "Works Cited" section contains complete bibliographic information for each work in the anthology, followed by the "Additional Recommended Books and Websites" section, for readers interested in learning more about the founders and their work.

Notes on Editing

Thirteen of the sixteen writings in this anthology were either originally published in English, e.g., those by Spencer, Mead, and Ward, or they were translated by others from French or German into English, e.g., those by Comte, Marx, and Tarde. The remaining three selections, by Durkheim, Tönnies, and Weber, were translated for this anthology. As regards the writings either originally published in English or translated by others into English, I have taken great care to present them as they appear in the source documents, to the maximum extent possible. It was necessary at times, however, to make certain edits to the text, in order to give modern readers a comprehensible, relevant experience, and also to give this book a uniformity of style. Thus, I made the following changes with regard to punctuation, spelling, word usage, deletions, emphasized words, and footnotes:

Punctuation: I have retained the punctuation in the source works, except in rare instances when it resulted in errors, such as run-on sentences or sentence fragments, which made comprehension difficult.

Spelling: I have corrected spelling errors contained in the source works and retained almost all British spellings of English words, such as "vigour," "analyse," and "practise," among many others.

Inconsistencies of style or word usage: In rare instances the authors used spellings or capitalization inconsistently, e.g., in the Comte selection, within a sentence the word "Theological" sometimes appears with a capital T and sometimes with a small t ("theological"). I have retained such inconsistencies in the source texts, because I did not feel any of them interfered with comprehension or readability.

Emphasized text: In some of the selections, the authors chose to call attention to words or phrases by using capitalization, italics, or other text attributes. I have retained such attributes and have not emphasized any text not emphasized in the source documents.

Deletions: In a few of the selections I have deleted the following: (a) an "outline" at the beginning of a chapter that some authors used to introduce the text that followed, which was a common device in nineteenth century books that served no particular substantive purpose; (b) "head quotations," which lead off some chapters, and are sometimes in a foreign language; (c) some text, including footnotes, in a few of the selections, for one of three reasons: (1) because the text was an "aside" to the main argument or content of the writing, which did not add anything to the main argument; (2) because the text contained examples that were so historically specific, concerning people, places, or events, that it would be unlikely to be known or relevant to modern readers; (3) because the points being made were redundant, i.e., stated more than once within the same article or book chapter. For example, the selection from Weber's *The Protestant Ethic and the Sprit of Capitalism* is presented without the footnotes because Weber appended them to later editions of the work in response to critics, and they are largely extraneous to the original work and irrelevant to modern readers in terms of content. (For more on these points see the "Introduction" to the second Roxbury Edition of *The Protestant Ethic* listed in the "Additional Recommended Books and Websites" section, especially pages xx and xxxvii.)

In no instance was text deleted that I felt would detract from the major contribution of the writer or the selection chosen for this anthology. When such text has been deleted from the body of a writing, it is indicated by an ellipsis in brackets, i.e., [. . .]

Uniformity of Appearance and Style: Each of the sixteen source documents in this anthology was originally published with different formatting and typestyles, of course, and the same is true of their subsequent reprintings in books and journals. To eliminate such variation and give this book a uniformity of appearance and style, I have presented all the selections with the same formatting and typeface attributes.

A Few Final Thoughts

Some of the selections in this anthology have a more "formal" feel than we are used to in much contemporary writing, e.g., in terms of their syntax and vocabulary, largely because they were written between about 1830 and 1920. When you come across such a selection, I suggest you read it more slowly, i.e., with a bit more patience, than you might read a less formal, more modern sounding text in this collection, to give yourself a chance to get acclimated to the style of writing.

No matter how you experience the style or "feel" of a given text, however, you may be surprised to see how pertinent every selection is for understanding modern societies and our own lives within them. In other words, these seminal works about conspicuous consumption, class conflict, the looking glass self, and other topics written decades ago may be "old" but they are not "dated."

With the above in mind, happy reading!

Auguste Comte

1798–1857

Source: *The Positive Philosophy of Auguste Comte* (1858 edition)
Selection: Chapter I: Introduction, pp. 25-37

Comte was a French philosopher, mathematician, and social theorist born in Montpellier, who is usually credited with coining the term "sociologie." *As a teen he abandoned his family's devout Catholicism and royalism, and in 1814 entered the* École Polytechnique, *where he proved himself to be a brilliant scientist. Over the next decade he developed* sociologie, *the "science of society," which he claimed could be studied through "positive" methods, such as observation and experimentation. While part of Comte's motivation may have been to try to remedy the social unrest that resulted from the French Revolution, he fervently believed it was time for humankind to abandon the "theological" and "metaphysical" stages of history, and to study society objectively. He presented his ideas most fully in the six-volume* Cours de Philosophie Positive *(*Course of Positive Philosophy*), written between 1830 and 1842 (which was first translated into English by Harriet Martineau in 1855). Anticipating scientists in our own time, Comte stressed the need for a "unified theory" that would encompass all the sciences, which he believed are interconnected like branches from the same tree trunk. To Comte, however, the science of society was the most complex of them all, and thus it was the last to develop. He viewed the "Positive" philosophy or method not only as a scientific way to study phenomena, but also as akin to a new religion destined to save humankind from itself. In Chapter I of his great work presented below, Comte refers to the study of "social phenomena," "social physics," and "social science"—phrases for what we today know as "sociology."*

*

A general statement of any system of philosophy may be either a sketch of a doctrine to be established, or a summary of a doctrine already established. If greater value belongs to the last, the first is still important, as characterizing from its origin the subject to be treated. In a case like the present, where the proposed study is vast and hitherto indeterminate, it is especially important that the field of research should be marked out with all possible accuracy. For this purpose, I will glance at the considerations which have originated this work, and which will be fully elaborated in the course of it.

In order to understand the true value and character of the Positive Philosophy, we must take a brief general view of the progressive course of the human mind, regarded as a whole; for no conception can be understood otherwise than through its history.

From the study of the development of human intelligence, in all directions, and through all times, the discovery arises of a great fundamental law, to which it is necessarily subject, and which has a solid foundation of proof, both in the facts of our organization and in our historical experience. The law is this:—that each of our leading conceptions, each branch of our knowledge—passes successively through three different theoretical conditions: the Theological, or fictitious; the Metaphysical, or abstract; and the Scientific, or positive. In other words, the human mind, by its nature, employs in its progress three methods of philosophizing, the character of which is essentially different, and even radically opposed: viz., the theological method, the metaphysical, and the positive. Hence arise three philosophies, or general systems of conceptions on the aggregate of phenomena, each of which excludes the others. The first is the necessary point of departure of the human understanding; and the third is its fixed and definite state. The second is merely a state of transition.

In the theological state, the human mind, seeking the essential nature of beings, the first and final causes (the origin and purpose) of all effects—in short, Absolute knowledge—supposes all phenomena to be produced by the immediate action of supernatural beings.

In the metaphysical state, which is only a modification of the first, the mind supposes, instead of supernatural beings, abstract forces, veritable entities (that is, personified abstractions) inherent in all beings, and capable of producing all phenomena. What is called the explanation of phenomena is, in this stage, a mere reference of each to its proper entity.

In the final, the positive state, the mind has given over the vain search after Absolute notions, the origin and destination of the universe, and the causes of phenomena, and applies itself to the study of their laws—that is, their invariable relations of succession and resemblance. Reasoning and observation, duly combined, are the means of this knowledge. What is now understood when we speak of an explanation of facts is simply the establishment of a connection between single phenomena and some general facts, the number of which continually diminishes with the progress of science.

The Theological system arrived at the highest perfection of which it is capable when it substituted the providential action of a single Being for the varied operations of the numerous divinities which had been before imagined. In the same way, in the last stage of the Metaphysical system, men substitute one great entity (Nature) as the cause of all phenomena, instead of the multitude of entities at first supposed. In the same way, again, the ultimate perfection of the Positive system would be (if such perfection could be hoped for) to represent all phenomena as particular aspects of a single general fact—such as Gravitation, for instance.

The importance of the working of this general law will be established hereafter. At present, it must suffice to point out some of the grounds of it.

There is no science which, having attained the positive stage, does not bear marks of having passed through the others. Some time since it was (whatever it might be) composed, as we can now perceive, of metaphysical abstractions; and, further back in the course of time, it took its form from theological conceptions. We shall have only too much occasion to see, as we proceed, that our most advanced sciences still bear very evident marks of the two earlier periods through which they have passed.

The progress of the individual mind is not only an illustration, but an indirect evidence of that of the general mind. The point of departure of the individual and of the race being the same, the phases of the mind of a man correspond to the epochs of the mind of the race. Now, each of us is aware, if he looks back upon his own history, that he was a theologian in his childhood, a metaphysician in his youth, and a natural philosopher in his manhood. All men who are up to their age can verify this for themselves.

Besides the observation of facts, we have theoretical reasons in support of this law. The most important of these reasons arises from the necessity that always exists for some theory to which to refer our facts, combined with the clear impossibility that, at the outset of human knowledge, men could have formed theories out of the observation of facts. All good intellects have repeated, since Bacon's time, that there can be no real knowledge but that which is based on observed facts. This is incontestable, in our present advanced stage; but, if we look back to the primitive stage of human knowledge, we shall see that it must have been otherwise then. If it is true that every theory must be based upon observed facts, it is equally true that facts can not be observed without the guidance of some theory. Without such guidance, our facts would be desultory and fruitless; we could not retain them: for the most part we could not even perceive them.

Thus, between the necessity of observing facts in order to form a theory, and having a theory in order to observe facts, the human mind would have been entangled in a vicious circle, but for the natural opening afforded by Theological conceptions. This is the fundamental reason for the theological character of the primitive philosophy. This necessity is confirmed by the perfect suitability of the theological philosophy to the earliest researches of the human mind. It is remarkable that the most inaccessible questions—those of the nature of beings, and the origin and purpose of phenomena—should be the first to occur in a primitive state, while those which are really within our reach are regarded as almost unworthy of serious study. The reason is evident enough:—that experience alone can teach us the measure of our powers; and if men had not begun by an exaggerated estimate of what they can do, they would never have done all that they are capable of. Our organization requires this. At such a period there could have been no reception of a positive philosophy, whose function is to discover the laws of phenomena, and whose leading characteristic it is to regard as interdicted to human reason those sublime mysteries which theology explains, even to their minutest details, with the most attractive facility. It is just so under a practical view of the nature of the researches with which men first occupied themselves. Such inquiries offered the powerful charm of unlimited empire over the external world—a world destined wholly for our use, and involved in every way with our existence. The theological philosophy presenting this view, administered exactly the stimulus necessary to incite the human mind to the irksome labor without which it could make no progress. We can now scarcely conceive of such a state of things, our reason having become sufficiently mature to enter upon laborious scientific researches, without needing any such stimulus as wrought upon the imaginations of astrologers and alchemists. We have motive enough in the hope of discovering the laws of phenomena, with a view to the confirmation or rejection of a theory. But it could not be so in the earliest days; and it is to the chimeras of astrology and alchemy that we owe the long series of observations and experiments on which our positive science is based. Kepler felt this on behalf of astronomy, and Berthollet on behalf of chemistry. Thus was a spontaneous philosophy, the theological, the only possible beginning, method, and provisional system, out of which the Positive philosophy could grow. It is easy, after this, to perceive how Metaphysical methods and doctrines must have afforded the means of transition from the one to the other.

The human understanding, slow in its advance, could not step at once from the theological into the positive philosophy. The two are so radically opposed, that an intermediate system of conceptions has been necessary to render the transition possible. It is only in doing this, that metaphysical conceptions have any utility whatever. In contemplating phenomena, men substitute for supernatural direction a corresponding entity. This entity may have been supposed to be derived from the supernatural action: but it is more easily lost sight of, leaving attention free from the facts themselves, till, at length, metaphysical agents have ceased to be anything more than the abstract names of phenomena. It is not easy to say by what other process than this our minds could have passed from supernatural considerations to natural; from the theological system to the positive.

The law of human development being thus established, let us consider what is the proper nature of the Positive Philosophy.

As we have seen, the first characteristic of the Positive Philosophy is that it regards all phenomena as subjected to invariable natural Laws. Our business is—seeing how vain is any research into what are called Causes, whether first or final—to pursue an accurate discovery of these Laws, with a view to reducing them to the smallest possible number. By speculating upon causes, we could solve no difficulty about origin and purpose. Our real business is to analyse accurately the circumstances of phenomena, and to connect them by the natural relations of succession and resemblance. [. . .]

Before ascertaining the stage which the Positive Philosophy has reached, we must bear in mind that the different kinds of our knowledge have passed through the three stages of progress at different rates, and have not therefore arrived at the same time. The rate of advance depends on the nature of the knowledge in question, so distinctly that, as we shall see hereafter, this consideration constitutes an accessory to the fundamental law of progress. Any kind of knowledge reaches the positive stage early in proportion to its generality, simplicity, and independence of other departments. Astronomical science, which is above all made up of facts that are general, simple, and independent of other sciences, arrived first; then terrestrial Physics; then Chemistry; and, at length, Physiology.

It is difficult to assign any precise date to this revolution in science. It may be said, like everything else, to have been always going on; and especially since the labors of Aristotle and the school of Alexandria; and then from the introduction of natural science into the West of Europe by the Arabs. But, if we must fix upon some marked period, to serve as a rallying point, it must be that,—about two centuries ago,—when the human mind was astir under the precepts of Bacon, the conceptions of Descartes, and the discoveries of Galileo. Then it was that the spirit of the Positive philosophy rose up in opposition to that of the superstitious and scholastic systems which had hitherto obscured the true character of all science. Since that date, the progress of the Positive philosophy, and the decline of the other two, have been so marked that no rational mind now doubts that the revolution is destined to go on to its completion—every branch of knowledge being, sooner or later, brought within the operation of Positive philosophy. This is not yet the case. Some are still lying outside: and not till they are brought in will the Positive philosophy possess that character of universality which is necessary to its definitive constitution.

In mentioning just now the four principal categories of phenomena,—astronomical, physical, chemical, and physiological,—there was an omission which will have been noticed. Nothing was said of Social phenomena. Though involved with the physiological, Social phenomena demand a distinct classification, both on account of their importance and of their difficulty. They are the most individual, the most complicated, the most dependent on all others; and therefore they must be the latest,—even if they had no special obstacle to encounter. This branch of science has not hitherto entered into the domain of Positive philosophy. Theological and metaphysical methods, exploded in other departments, are as yet exclusively applied, both in the way of inquiry and discussion, in all treatment of Social subjects, though the best minds are heartily weary of eternal disputes about divine right and the sovereignty of the people. This is the great, while it is evidently the only gap which has to be filled, to constitute, solid and entire, the Positive Philosophy. Now that the human mind has grasped celestial and terrestrial physics,—mechanical and chemical; organic physics, both vegetable and animal,—there remains one science to fill up the series of sciences of observation,—Social physics. This is what men have now most need of: and this it is the principal aim of the present work to establish.

It would be absurd to pretend to offer this new science at once in a complete state. Others, less new, are in very unequal conditions of forwardness. But the same character of positivity which is impressed on all the others will be shown to belong to this. This once done, the philosophical system of the moderns will be in fact complete, as there will then be no phenomenon which does not naturally enter into some one of the five great categories. All our fundamental conceptions having become homogeneous, the Positive state will be fully established. It can never again change its character, though it will be for ever in course of development by additions of new knowledge. Having acquired the character of universality which has hitherto been the only advantage resting with the two preceding systems, it will supersede them by its natural superiority, and leave to them only an historical existence.

We have stated the special aim of this work. Its secondary and general aim is this:—to review what has been effected in the Sciences, in order to show that they are not radically separate, but all branches from the same trunk. If we had confined ourselves to the first and special object of the work, we should have produced merely a study of Social physics: whereas, in introducing the second and general, we offer study of Positive philosophy,—passing in review all the positive sciences already formed.

The purpose of this work is not to give an account of the Natural Sciences. Besides that it would be endless, and that it would require a scientific preparation such as no one man possesses, it would be apart from our object, which is to go through a course of not Positive Science, but Positive Philosophy. We have only to consider each fundamental science in its relation to the whole positive system, and to the spirit which characterizes it; that is, with regard to its methods and its chief results.

The two aims, though distinct, are inseparable; for, on the one hand, there can be no positive philosophy without a basis of social science, without which it could not be all-comprehensive; and, on the other hand, we could not pursue Social science without having been prepared by the study of phenomena less complicated than those of society, and furnished with a knowledge of laws and anterior facts which have a bearing upon social science. Though the fundamental sciences are not all equally interesting to ordinary minds, there is no one of them that can be neglected in an inquiry like the present; and, in the eye of philosophy, all are of equal value to human welfare. Even those which appear the least interesting have their own value, either on account of the perfection of their methods, or as being the necessary basis of all the others.

Lest it should be supposed that our course will lead us into a wilderness of such special studies as are at present the bane of a true positive philosophy, we will briefly advert to the existing prevalence of such special pursuit. In the primitive state of human knowledge there is no regular division of intellectual labor. Every student cultivates all the sciences. As knowledge accrues, the sciences part off; and students devote themselves each to some one branch. It is owing to this division of employment, and concentration of whole minds upon a single department, that science has made so prodigious an advance in modern times; and the perfection of this division is one of the most important characteristics of the Positive philosophy. But, while admitting all the merits of this change, we can not be blind to the eminent disadvantages which arise from the limitation of minds to a particular study. It is inevitable that each should be possessed with exclusive notions, and be therefore incapable of the general superiority of ancient students, who actually owed that general superiority to the inferiority of their knowledge. We must consider whether the evil can be avoided without losing the good of the modern arrangement; for the evil is becoming urgent. We all acknowledge that the divisions established for the convenience of scientific pursuit are radically artificial; and yet there are very few who can embrace in idea the whole of any one science: each science moreover being itself only a part of a great whole. Almost every one is busy about his own particular section without much thought about its relation to the general system of positive knowledge. We must not be blind to the evil, nor slow in seeking a remedy. We must not forget that this is the weak side of the positive philosophy, by which it may yet be attacked, with some hope of success, by the adherents of the theological and metaphysical systems. As to the remedy, it certainly does not lie in a return to the ancient confusion of pursuits, which would be mere retrogression, if it were possible, which it is not. It lies in perfecting the division of employments itself,—in carrying it one degree higher,—in constituting one more specialty from the study of scientific generalities.

Let us have a new class of students, suitably prepared, whose business it shall be to take the respective sciences as they are, determine the spirit of each, ascertain their relations and mutual connection, and reduce their respective principles to the smallest number of general principles, in conformity with the fundamental rules of the Positive Method. At the same time, let other students be prepared for their special pursuit by an education which recognises the whole scope of positive science, so as to profit by the labors of the students of generalities and so as to correct reciprocally, under that guidance, the results obtained by each. We see some approach already to this arrangement. Once established, there would be nothing to apprehend from any extent of division of employments. When we once have a class of learned men, at the disposal of all others, whose business it shall be to connect each new discovery with the general system, we may dismiss all fear of the great whole being lost sight of in the pursuit of the details of knowledge. The organization of scientific research will then be complete; and it will henceforth have occasion only to extend its development, and not to change its character. After all, the formation of such a new class as is proposed would be merely an extension of the principle which has created all the classes we have. While science was narrow, there was only one class: as it expanded, more were instituted. With a further advance a fresh need arises, and this new class will be the result. [. . .]

Now, the existing disorder is abundantly accounted for by the existence, all at once, of three incompatible philosophies—the theological, the metaphysical, and the positive. Any one of these might alone secure some sort of social order; but while the three co-exist, it is impossible for us to understand one another upon any essential point whatever. If this is true, we have only to ascertain which of the philosophies must, in the nature of things, prevail; and, this ascertained, every man, whatever may have been his former views, can not but concur in its triumph. The problem once recognised, can not remain long unsolved; for all considerations whatever point to the Positive Philosophy as the one destined to prevail. It alone has been advancing during a course of centuries throughout which the others have been declining. The fact is incontestable. Some may deplore it, but none can destroy it, nor therefore neglect it but under penalty of being betrayed by illusory speculations. This general revolution of the human mind is nearly accomplished. We have only to complete the Positive Philosophy by bringing Social phenomena within its comprehension, and afterward consolidating the whole into one body of homogeneous doctrine. The marked preference which almost all minds, from the highest to the commonest, accord to positive knowledge over vague and mystical conceptions, is a pledge of what the reception of this philosophy will be when it has acquired the only quality that it now wants—a character of due generality. When it has become complete, its supremacy will take place spontaneously and will re-establish order throughout society. There is at present no conflict but between the theological and the metaphysical philosophies. They are contending for the task of reorganizing society; but it is a work too mighty for either of them. The positive philosophy has hitherto intervened only to examine both, and both are abundantly discredited by the process. It is time now to be doing something more effective, without wasting our forces in needless controversy. It is time to complete the vast intellectual operation begun by Bacon, Descartes, and Galileo, by constructing the system of general ideas which must henceforth prevail among the human race. This is the way to put an end to the revolutionary crisis which is tormenting the civilized nations of the world.

Karl Marx

1818-1883

Source: *The Manifesto of the Communist Party*
(with Frederick Engels) (1906 edition)
Selection: Bourgeois and Proletarians, pp. 12-32

The German philosopher, economist, political revolutionary, and utopian thinker Karl Marx is considered one of the "holy trinity" of sociology (along with Durkheim and Weber). After studying law, getting a doctorate degree, and working as a journalist, he become heavily influenced by the writings of the philosopher Hegel and actively involved with the socialist movements in the mid-nineteenth century, when masses of people were living in subhuman conditions. Over his lifetime, Marx wrote many seminal works that influenced millions of people around the world, including Economic and Philosophic Manuscripts, Das Kapital, *and* The Manifesto of the Communist Party (*commonly called* The Communist Manifesto). *Collectively, his books analyzed such fundamental subject matter as capitalism, alienation, social class, class conflict, and dialectical materialism. In* The Communist Manifesto, *written with Frederick Engels in late 1847 and published in 1848, these concepts are concisely and brilliantly discussed in the service of a revolutionary call to action. As stated in the Preface, the* Manifesto *was published as the platform of the Communist League, a working men's association, first exclusively German and later international. Below is the opening section, "Bourgeois and Proletarians," which analyzes the conflict between the "two great hostile camps" and the ultimate solution to the conflict through the process of dialectical materialism.*

*

Bourgeois and Proletarians[1]. The history of all hitherto existing society[2] is the history of class struggles.

Freeman and slave, patrician and plebian, lord and serf, guild-master[3] and journeyman, in a word, oppressor and oppressed, stood in constant opposition to one another, carried on an uninterrupted, now hidden, now open fight, a fight that each time ended either in a revolutionary reconstitution of society at large, or in the common ruin of the contending classes.

In the earlier epochs of history, we find almost everywhere a complicated arrangement of society into various orders, a manifold gradation of social rank. In ancient Rome we have patricians, knights, plebians, slaves; in the Middle Ages, feudal lords, vassals, guild-masters, journeymen, apprentices, serfs; in almost all of these classes, again, subordinate gradations.

The modern bourgeois society that has sprouted from the ruins of feudal society has not done away with class antagonisms. It has but established new classes, new conditions of oppression, new forms of struggle in place of the old ones.

Our epoch, the epoch of the bourgeoisie, possesses, however, this distinct feature: it has simplified class antagonisms. Society as a whole is more and more splitting up into two great hostile camps, into two great classes directly facing each other—bourgeoisie and proletariat.

From the serfs of the Middle Ages sprang the chartered burghers of the earliest towns. From these burgesses the first elements of the bourgeoisie were developed.

The discovery of America, the rounding of the Cape, opened up fresh ground for the rising bourgeoisie. The East-Indian and Chinese markets, the colonisation of America, trade with the colonies, the increase in the means of exchange and in commodities generally, gave to commerce, to navigation, to industry, an impulse never before known, and thereby, to the revolutionary element in the tottering feudal society, a rapid development.

The feudal system of industry, in which industrial production was monopolized by closed guilds, now no longer suffices for the growing wants of the new markets. The manufacturing system took its place. The guild-masters were pushed aside by the manufacturing middle class; division of labor between the different corporate guilds vanished in the face of division of labor in each single workshop.

Meantime, the markets kept ever growing, the demand ever rising. Even manufacturers no longer sufficed. Thereupon, steam and machinery revolutionized industrial production. The place of manufacture was taken by the giant, MODERN INDUSTRY; the place of the industrial middle class by industrial millionaires, the leaders of the whole industrial armies, the modern bourgeois.

Modern industry has established the world market, for which the discovery of America paved the way. This market has given an immense development to commerce, to navigation, to communication by land. This development has, in turn, reacted on the extension of industry; and in proportion as industry, commerce, navigation, railways extended, in the same proportion the bourgeoisie developed, increased its capital, and pushed into the background every class handed down from the Middle Ages.

We see, therefore, how the modern bourgeoisie is itself the product of a long course of development, of a series of revolutions in the modes of production and of exchange.

Each step in the development of the bourgeoisie was accompanied by a corresponding political advance in that class. An oppressed class under the sway of the feudal nobility, an armed and self-governing association of medieval commune[4]: here independent urban republic (as in Italy and Germany); there taxable "third estate" of the monarchy (as in France); afterward, in the period of manufacturing proper, serving either the semi-feudal or the absolute monarchy as a counterpoise against the nobility, and, in fact, cornerstone of the great monarchies in general—the bourgeoisie has at last, since the establishment of Modern Industry and of the world market, conquered for itself, in the modern representative state, exclusive political sway. The executive of the modern state is but a committee for managing the common affairs of the whole bourgeoisie.

The bourgeoisie, historically, has played a most revolutionary part.

The bourgeoisie, wherever it has got the upper hand, has put an end to all feudal, patriarchal, idyllic relations. It has pitilessly torn asunder the motley feudal ties that bound man to his "natural superiors," and has left no other nexus between man and man than naked self-interest, than callous "cash payment." It has drowned out the most heavenly ecstasies of religious fervor, of chivalrous enthusiasm, of philistine sentimentalism, in the icy water of egotistical calculation. It has resolved personal worth into exchange value, and in place of the numberless indefeasible chartered freedoms, has set up that single, unconscionable freedom—Free Trade. In one word, for exploitation, veiled by religious and political illusions, it has substituted naked, shameless, direct, brutal exploitation.

The bourgeoisie has stripped of its halo every occupation hitherto honored and looked up to with reverent awe. It has converted the physician, the lawyer, the priest, the poet, the man of science, into its paid wage laborers.

The bourgeoisie has torn away from the family its sentimental veil, and has reduced the family relation into a mere money relation.

The bourgeoisie has disclosed how it came to pass that the brutal display of vigor in the Middle Ages, which reactionaries so much admire, found its fitting complement in the most slothful indolence. It has been the first to show what man's activity can bring about. It has accomplished wonders far surpassing Egyptian pyramids, Roman aqueducts, and Gothic cathedrals; it has conducted expeditions that put in the shade all former exoduses of nations and crusades.

The bourgeoisie cannot exist without constantly revolutionizing the instruments of production, and thereby the relations of production, and with them the whole relations of society. Conservation of the old modes of production in unaltered form was, on the contrary, the first condition of existence for all earlier industrial classes. Constant revolutionizing of production, uninterrupted disturbance of all social conditions, everlasting uncertainty and agitation distinguish the bourgeois epoch from all earlier ones. All fixed, fast frozen relations, with their train of ancient and venerable prejudices and opinions, are swept away, all new-formed ones become antiquated before they can ossify. All that is solid melts into air, all that is holy is profaned, and man is at last compelled to face with sober senses his real condition of life and his relations with his kind.

The need of a constantly expanding market for its products chases the bourgeoisie over the entire surface of the globe. It must nestle everywhere, settle everywhere, establish connections everywhere.

The bourgeoisie has, through its exploitation of the world market, given a cosmopolitan character to production and consumption in every country. To the great chagrin of reactionaries, it has drawn from under the feet of industry the national ground on which it stood. All old-established national industries have been destroyed or are daily being destroyed. They are dislodged by new industries, whose introduction becomes a life and death question for all civilized nations, by industries that no longer work up indigenous raw material, but raw material drawn from the remotest zones; industries whose products are consumed, not only at home, but in every quarter of the globe. In place of the old wants, satisfied by the production of the country, we find new wants, requiring for their satisfaction the products of distant lands and climes. In place of the old local and national seclusion and self-sufficiency, we have intercourse in every direction, universal inter-dependence of nations. And as in material, so also in intellectual production. The intellectual creations of individual nations become common property. National one-sidedness and narrow-mindedness become more and more impossible, and from the numerous national and local literatures, there arises a world literature.

The bourgeoisie, by the rapid improvement of all instruments of production, by the immensely facilitated means of communication, draws all, even the most barbarian, nations into civilization. The cheap prices of commodities are the heavy artillery with which it forces the barbarians' intensely obstinate hatred of foreigners to capitulate. It compels all nations, on pain of extinction, to adopt the bourgeois mode of production; it compels them to introduce what it calls civilization into their midst, i.e., to become bourgeois themselves. In one word, it creates a world after its own image.

The bourgeoisie has subjected the country to the rule of the towns. It has created enormous cities, has greatly increased the urban population as compared with the rural, and has thus rescued a considerable part of the population from the idiocy of rural life. Just as it has made the country dependent on the towns, so it has made barbarian and semi-barbarian countries dependent on the civilized ones, nations of peasants on nations of bourgeois, the East on the West.

The bourgeoisie keeps more and more doing away with the scattered state of the population, of the means of production, and of property. It has agglomerated population, centralized the means of production, and has concentrated property in a few hands. The necessary consequence of this was political centralization. Independent, or but loosely connected provinces, with separate interests, laws, governments, and systems of taxation, became lumped together into one nation, with one government, one code of laws, one national class interest, one frontier, and one customs tariff.

The bourgeoisie, during its rule of scarce one hundred years, has created more massive and more colossal productive forces than have all preceding generations together. Subjection of nature's forces to man, machinery, application of chemistry to industry and agriculture, steam navigation, railways, electric telegraphs, clearing of whole continents for cultivation, canalization or rivers, whole populations conjured out of the ground—what earlier century had even a presentiment that such productive forces slumbered in the lap of social labor?

We see then: the means of production and of exchange, on whose foundation the bourgeoisie built itself up, were generated in feudal society. At a certain stage in the development of these means of production and of exchange, the conditions under which feudal society produced and exchanged, the feudal organization of agriculture and manufacturing industry, in one word, the feudal relations of property became no longer compatible with the already developed productive forces; they became so many fetters. They had to be burst asunder; they were burst asunder.

Into their place stepped free competition, accompanied by a social and political constitution adapted in it, and the economic and political sway of the bourgeois class.

A similar movement is going on before our own eyes. Modern bourgeois society, with its relations of production, of exchange and of property, a society that has conjured up such gigantic means of production and of exchange, is like the sorcerer who is no longer able to control the powers of the nether world whom he has called up by his spells. For many a decade past, the history of industry and commerce is but the history of the revolt of modern productive forces against modern conditions of production, against the property relations that are the conditions for the existence of the bourgeois and of its rule. It is enough to mention the commercial crises that, by their periodical return, put the existence of the entire bourgeois society on its trial, each time more threateningly. In these crises, a great part not only of the existing products, but also of the previously created productive forces, are periodically destroyed. In these crises, there breaks out an epidemic that, in all earlier epochs, would have seemed an absurdity—the epidemic of over-production. Society suddenly finds itself put back into a state of momentary barbarism; it appears as if a famine, a universal war of devastation, had cut off the supply of every means of subsistence; industry and commerce seem to be destroyed. And why? Because there is too much civilization, too much means of subsistence, too much industry, too much commerce. The productive forces at the disposal of society no longer tend to further the development of the conditions of bourgeois property; on the contrary, they have become too powerful for these conditions, by which they are fettered, and so soon as they overcome these fetters, they bring disorder into the whole of bourgeois society, endanger the existence of bourgeois property. The conditions of bourgeois society are too narrow to comprise the wealth created by them. And how does the bourgeoisie get over these crises? On the one hand, by enforced destruction of a mass of productive forces; on the other, by the conquest of new markets, and by the more thorough exploitation of the old ones. That is to say, by paving the way for more extensive and more destructive crises, and by diminishing the means whereby crises are prevented.

The weapons with which the bourgeoisie felled feudalism to the ground are now turned against the bourgeoisie itself.

But not only has the bourgeoisie forged the weapons that bring death to itself; it has also called into existence the men who are to wield those weapons—the modern working class—the proletarians.

In proportion as the bourgeoisie, i.e., capital, is developed, in the same proportion is the proletariat, the modern working class, developed—a class of laborers, who live only so long as they find work, and who find work only so long as their labor increases capital. These laborers, who must sell themselves piecemeal, are a commodity, like every other article of commerce, and are consequently exposed to all the vicissitudes of competition, to all the fluctuations of the market.

Owing to the extensive use of machinery, and to the division of labor, the work of the proletarians has lost all individual character, and, consequently, all charm for the workman. He becomes an appendage of the machine, and it is only the most simple, most monotonous, and most easily acquired knack, that is required of him. Hence, the cost of production of a workman is restricted, almost entirely, to the means of subsistence that he requires for maintenance, and for the propagation of his race. But the price of a commodity, and therefore also of labor, is equal to its cost of production. In proportion, therefore, as the repulsiveness of the work increases, the wage decreases. What is more, in proportion as the use of machinery and division of labor increases, in the same proportion the burden of toil also increases, whether by prolongation of the working hours, by the increase of the work exacted in a given time, or by increased speed of machinery, etc.

Modern Industry has converted the little workshop of the patriarchal master into the great factory of the industrial capitalist. Masses of laborers, crowded into the factory, are organized like soldiers. As privates of the industrial army, they are placed under the command of a perfect hierarchy of officers and sergeants. Not only are they slaves of the bourgeois class, and of the bourgeois state; they are daily and hourly enslaved by the machine, by the overlooker, and, above all, in the individual bourgeois manufacturer himself. The more openly this despotism proclaims gain to be its end and aim, the more petty, the more hateful and the more embittering it is.

The less the skill and exertion of strength implied in manual labor, in other words, the more modern industry becomes developed, the more is the labor of men superseded by that of women. Differences of age and sex have no longer any distinctive social validity for the working class.

All are instruments of labor, more or less expensive to use, according to their age and sex.

No sooner is the exploitation of the laborer by the manufacturer so far at an end that he receives his wages in cash, than he is set upon by the other portion of the bourgeoisie, the landlord, the shopkeeper, the pawnbroker, etc.

The lower strata of the middle class—the small tradespeople, shopkeepers, and retired tradesmen generally, the handicraftsmen and peasants—all these sink gradually into the proletariat, partly because their diminutive capital does not suffice for the scale on which Modern Industry is carried on, and is swamped in the competition with the large capitalists, partly because their specialized skill is rendered worthless by new methods of production. Thus, the proletariat is recruited from all classes of the population.

The proletariat goes through various stages of development. With its birth begins its struggle with the bourgeoisie. At first, the contest is carried on by individual laborers, then by the work of people of a factory, then by the operative of one trade, in one locality, against the individual bourgeois who directly exploits them. They direct their attacks not against the bourgeois condition of production, but against the instruments of production themselves; they destroy imported wares that compete with their labor, they smash to pieces machinery, they set factories ablaze, they seek to restore by force the vanished status of the workman of the Middle Ages.

At this stage, the laborers still form an incoherent mass scattered over the whole country, and broken up by their mutual competition. If anywhere they unite to form more compact bodies, this is not yet the consequence of their own active union, but of the union of the bourgeoisie, which class, in order to attain its own political ends, is compelled to set the whole proletariat in motion, and is moreover yet, for a time, able to do so. At this stage, therefore, the proletarians do not fight their enemies, but the enemies of their enemies, the remnants of absolute monarchy, the landowners, the non-industrial bourgeois, the petty bourgeois. Thus, the whole historical movement is concentrated in the hands of the bourgeoisie; every victory so obtained is a victory for the bourgeoisie.

But with the development of industry, the proletariat not only increases in number; it becomes concentrated in greater masses, its strength grows, and it feels that strength more. The various interests and conditions of life within the ranks of the proletariat are more and more equalized, in proportion as machinery obliterates all distinctions of labor, and nearly everywhere reduces wages to the same low level. The growing competition among the bourgeois, and the resulting commercial crises, make the wages of the workers ever more fluctuating. The increasing improvement of machinery, ever more rapidly developing, makes their livelihood more and more precarious; the collisions between individual workmen and individual bourgeois take more and more the character of collisions between two classes. Thereupon, the workers begin to form combinations (trade unions) against the bourgeois; they club together in order to keep up the rate of wages; they found permanent associations in order to make provision beforehand for these occasional revolts. Here and there, the contest breaks out into riots.

Now and then the workers are victorious, but only for a time. The real fruit of their battles lie not in the immediate result, but in the ever expanding union of the workers. This union is helped on by the improved means of communication that are created by Modern Industry, and that place the workers of different localities in contact with one another. It was just this contact that was needed to centralize the numerous local struggles, all of the same character, into one national struggle between classes. But every class struggle is a political struggle. And that union, to attain which the burghers of the Middle Ages, with their miserable highways, required centuries, the modern proletarian, thanks to railways, achieve in a few years.

This organization of the proletarians into a class, and, consequently, into a political party, is continually being upset again by the competition between the workers themselves. But it ever rises up again, stronger, firmer, mightier. It compels legislative recognition of particular interests of the workers, by taking advantage of the divisions among the bourgeoisie itself. Thus, the Ten-Hours Bill in England was carried.

Altogether, collisions between the classes of the old society further in many ways the course of development of the proletariat. The bourgeoisie finds itself involved in a constant battle. At first with the aristocracy; later on, with those portions of the bourgeoisie itself, whose interests have become antagonistic to the progress of industry; at all time with the bourgeoisie of foreign countries. In all these battles, it sees itself compelled to appeal to the proletariat, to ask for help, and thus to drag it into the political arena. The bourgeoisie itself, therefore, supplies the proletariat with its own elements of political and general education, in other words, it furnishes the proletariat with weapons for fighting the bourgeoisie.

Further, as we have already seen, entire sections of the ruling class are, by the advance of industry, precipitated into the proletariat, or are at least threatened in their conditions of existence. These also supply the proletariat with fresh elements of enlightenment and progress.

Finally, in times when the class struggle nears the decisive hour, the progress of dissolution going on within the ruling class, in fact within the whole range of old society, assumes such a violent, glaring character, that a small section of the ruling class cuts itself adrift, and joins the revolutionary class, the class that holds the future in its hands. Just as, therefore, at an earlier period, a section of the nobility went over to the bourgeoisie, so now a portion of the bourgeoisie goes over to the proletariat and in particular, a portion of the bourgeois ideologists, who have raised themselves to the level of comprehending theoretically the historical movement as a whole.

Of all the classes that stand face to face with the bourgeoisie today, the proletariat alone is a genuinely revolutionary class. The other classes decay and finally disappear in the face of Modern Industry; the proletariat is its special and essential product.

The lower middle class, the small manufacturer, the shopkeeper, the artisan, the peasant, all these fight against the bourgeoisie, to save from extinction their existence as fractions of the middle class. They are therefore not revolutionary, but conservative. Nay, more, they are reactionary, for they try to roll back the wheel of history. If, by chance, they are revolutionary, they are only so in view of their impending transfer into the proletariat; they thus defend not their present, but their future interests; they desert their own standpoint to place themselves at that of the proletariat.

The "dangerous class," the social scum, that passively rotting mass thrown off by the lowest layers of the old society, may, here and there, be swept into the movement by a proletarian revolution; its conditions of life, however, prepare it far more for the part of a bribed tool of reactionary intrigue.

In the condition of the proletariat, those of old society at large are already virtually swamped. The proletarian is without property; his relation to his wife and children has no longer anything in common with the bourgeois family relations; modern industry labor, modern subjection to capital, the same in England as in France, in America as in Germany, has stripped him of every trace of national character. Law, morality, religion, are to him so many bourgeois prejudices, behind which lurk in ambush just as many bourgeois interests.

All the preceding classes that got the upper hand sought to fortify their already acquired status by subjecting society at large to their conditions of appropriation. The proletarians cannot become masters of the productive forces of society, except by abolishing their own previous mode of appropriation, and thereby also every other previous mode of appropriation. They have nothing of their own to secure and to fortify; their mission is to destroy all previous securities for, and insurances of, individual property.

All previous historical movements were movements of minorities, or in the interest of minorities. The proletarian movement is the self-conscious, independent movement of the immense majority, in the interest of the immense majority. The proletariat, the lowest stratum of our present society, cannot stir, cannot raise itself up, without the whole superincumbent strata of official society being sprung into the air.

Though not in substance, yet in form, the struggle of the proletariat with the bourgeoisie is at first a national struggle. The proletariat of each country must, of course, first of all settle matters with its own bourgeoisie.

In depicting the most general phases of the development of the proletariat, we traced the more or less veiled civil war, raging within existing society, up to the point where that war breaks out into open revolution, and where the violent overthrow of the bourgeoisie lays the foundation for the sway of the proletariat.

Hitherto, every form of society has been based, as we have already seen, on the antagonism of oppressing and oppressed classes. But in order to oppress a class, certain conditions must be assured to it under which it can, at least, continue its slavish existence. The serf, in the period of serfdom, raised himself to membership in the commune, just as the petty bourgeois, under the yoke of the feudal absolutism, managed to develop into a bourgeois. The modern laborer, on the contrary, instead of rising with the process of industry, sinks deeper and deeper below the conditions of existence of his own class. He becomes a pauper, and pauperism develops more rapidly than population and wealth. And here it becomes evident that the bourgeoisie is unfit any longer to be the ruling class in society, and to impose its conditions of existence upon society as an overriding law. It is unfit to rule because it is incompetent to assure an existence to its slave within his slavery, because it cannot help letting him sink into such a state, that it has to feed him, instead of being fed by him. Society can no longer live under this bourgeoisie, in other words, its existence is no longer compatible with society.

The essential conditions for the existence and for the sway of the bourgeois class is the formation and augmentation of capital; the condition for capital is wage labor. Wage labor rests exclusively on competition between the laborers. The advance of industry, whose involuntary promoter is the bourgeoisie, replaces the isolation of the laborers, due to competition, by the revolutionary combination, due to association. The development of Modern Industry, therefore, cuts from under its feet the very foundation on which the bourgeoisie produces and appropriates products. What the bourgeoisie therefore produces, above all, are its own grave-diggers. Its fall and the victory of the proletariat are equally inevitable.

Footnotes

[1] By bourgeoisie is meant the class of modern capitalists, owners of the means of social production and employers of wage labor. By proletariat, the class of modern wage laborers who, having no means of production of their own, are reduced to selling their labor power in order to live.

[2] That is, all *written* history. In 1847, the pre-history of society, the social organization existing previous to recorded history, all but unknown. Since then, August von Haxthausen (1792-1866) discovered common ownership of land in Russia, Georg Ludwig von Maurer proved it to be the social foundation from which all Teutonic races started in history, and, by and by, village communities were found to be, or to have been, the primitive form of society everywhere from India to Ireland. The inner organization of this primitive communistic society was laid bare, in its typical form, by Lewis Henry Morgan's (1818-1861) crowning discovery of the true nature of the gens and its relation to the tribe. With the dissolution of the primeaval communities, society begins to be differentiated into separate and finally antagonistic classes. I have attempted to retrace this dissolution in *Der Ursprung der Familie, des Privateigenthumus und des Staats*, second edition, Stuttgart, 1886.

[3] Guild-master, that is, a full member of a guild, a master within, not a head of a guild.

[4] This was the name given their urban communities by the townsmen of Italy and France, after they had purchased or conquered their initial rights of self-government from their feudal lords. "Commune" was the name taken in France by the nascent towns even before they had conquered from their feudal lords and masters local self-government and political rights as the "Third Estate". Generally speaking, for the economical development of the bourgeoisie, England is here taken as the typical country, for its political development, France.

Herbert Spencer

1820-1903

Source: *The Study of Sociology* (1906 edition)
Selection: Chapter III: Nature of the Social Science, pp. 45-59

The English philosopher, engineer, political economist, and sociological theorist Herbert Spencer was one of the first major thinkers to use the term "sociology" in his writings. Despite his prolific output and contribution to many fields of study during the Victorian Era, Spencer is perhaps best remembered as the inventor of the phrase "survival of the fittest," reflecting his interest in Darwinian evolutionary theory, which he applied to society. In 1852, Spencer wrote an article defending biological evolution, before Darwin published his famous Origin of the Species, *and extended the evolutionary perspective into the realms of sociology and ethics. Because of his beliefs in the Darwinian conception of "natural selection" and the "survival of the fittest," Spencer is often referred to as the father of "Social Darwinism," which essentially promotes the view that the fittest or strongest in society should be those who survive and flourish. In the following selection from* The Study of Sociology, *first published in 1873, we see how Spencer discusses the infant discipline of sociology, distinguishes it from other scientific fields of study, and uses the biological organism as a model for how to think about and analyze the structure and function of human societies.*

*

Those who have been brought up in the belief that there is one law for the rest of the Universe and another law for mankind, will doubtless be astonished by the proposal to include aggregates of men in this generalization. And yet that the properties of the units determine the properties of the whole they make up, evidently holds of societies as of other things. A general survey of tribes and nations, past and present, shows clearly enough that it is so; and a brief consideration of the conditions shows, with no less clearness, that it must be so.

Ignoring for the moment the special traits of races and individuals, observe the traits common to members of the species at large; and consider how these must affect their relations when associated.

They have all needs for food, and have corresponding desires. To all of them exertion is a physiological expense; must bring a certain return in nutriment, if it is not to be detrimental; and is accompanied by repugnance when pushed to excess, or even before reaching it. They are all of them liable to bodily injury, with accompanying pain, from various extreme physical actions; and they are liable to emotional pains, of positive and negative kinds, from one another's actions. As says Shylock, insisting on that human nature which Jews have in common with Christians—

> "Hath not a Jew eyes? hath not a Jew hands, organs, dimensions, senses, affections, passions? fed with the same food, hurt with the same weapons, subject to the same diseases, healed by the same means, warmed and cooled by the same winter and summer, as a Christian is? If you prick us, do we not bleed? if you tickle us, do we not laugh? if you poison us, do we not die? and if you wrong us, shall we not revenge? If we are like you in the rest, we will resemble you in that."

Conspicuous, however, as is this possession of certain fundamental qualities by all individuals, there is no adequate recognition of the truth that from these individual qualities must result certain qualities in an assemblage of individuals; that in proportion as the individuals forming one assemblage are like in their qualities to the individuals forming another assemblage, the two assemblages will have likenesses; and that the assemblages will differ in their characters in proportion as the component individuals of the one differ from those of the other. Yet when this, which is almost a truism, has been admitted, it cannot be denied that in every community there is a group of phenomena growing naturally out of the phenomena presented by its members—a set of properties in the aggregate determined by the sets of properties in the units; and that the relations of the two sets form the subject-matter of a science. It needs but to ask what would happen if men avoided one another, as various inferior creatures do, to see that the very possibility of a society depends on a certain emotional property in the individual. It needs but to ask what would happen if each man liked best the men who gave him most pain, to perceive that social relations, supposing them to be possible, would be utterly unlike the social relations resulting from the greater liking which men individually have for others who give them pleasure. It needs but to ask what would happen if, instead of ordinarily preferring the easiest ways of achieving their ends, men preferred to achieve their ends in the most troublesome ways, to infer that then, a society, if one could exist, would be a widely-different society from any we know. And if, as these extreme cases show us, cardinal traits in societies are determined by cardinal traits in men, it cannot be questioned that less-marked traits in societies are determined by less-marked traits in men; and that there must everywhere be a consensus between the special structures and actions of the one and the special structures and actions of the other.

Setting out, then, with this general principle, that the properties of the units determine the properties of the aggregate, we conclude that there must be a Social Science expressing the relations between the two, with as much definiteness as the natures of the phenomena permit. Beginning with types of men who form but small and incoherent social aggregates, such a science has to show in what ways the individual qualities, intellectual and emotional, negate further aggregation. It has to explain how slight modifications of individual nature, arising under modified conditions of life, make somewhat larger aggregates possible. It has to trace out, in aggregates of some size, the genesis of the social relations, regulative and operative, into which the members fall. It has to exhibit the stronger and more prolonged social influences which, by further modifying the characters of the units, facilitate further aggregation with consequent further complexity of social structure.

Among societies of all orders and sizes, from the smallest and rudest up to the largest and most civilized, it has to ascertain what traits there are in common, determined by the common traits of human beings; what less-general traits, distinguishing certain groups of societies, result from traits distinguishing certain races of men; and what peculiarities in each society are traceable to the peculiarities of its members. In every case it has for its subject-matter the growth, development, structure, and functions of the social aggregate, as brought about by the mutual actions of individuals whose natures are partly like those of all men, partly like those of kindred races, partly distinctive.

These phenomena of social evolution have, of course, to be explained with due reference to the conditions each society is exposed to—the conditions furnished by its locality and by its relations to neighbouring societies. Noting this merely to prevent possible misapprehensions, the fact which here concerns us is not that the Social Science exhibits these or those special truths, but that given men having certain properties, and an aggregate of such men must have certain derivative properties which form the subject-matter of a science.

"But were we not told some pages back, that in societies, causes and effects are related in ways so involved that prevision is often impossible? Were we not warned against rashly taking measures for achieving this or that desideratum, regardless of the proofs, so abundantly supplied by the past, that agencies set in action habitually work out results never foreseen? And were not instances given of all-important changes that were due to influences from which no one would have anticipated them? If so, how can there be a Social Science? If Louis Napoleon could not have expected that the war he began to prevent the consolidation of Germany, would be the very means of consolidating it; if to M. Thiers, five-and-twenty years ago, it would have seemed a dream exceeding all ordinary dreams in absurdity, that he would be fired at from his own fortifications; how in the name of wonder is it possible to formulate social phenomena in anything approaching scientific order?"

The difficulty thus put in as strong a form as I can find for it, is that which, clearly or vaguely, rises in the minds of most to whom Sociology is proposed as a subject to be studied after scientific methods, with the expectation of reaching results having scientific certainty. Before giving to the question its special answer, let me give it a general answer.

The science of Mechanics has reached a development higher than has been reached by any but the purely-abstract sciences. Though we may not call it perfect, yet the great accuracy of the predictions which its ascertained principles enable astronomers to make, shows how near to perfection it has come; and the achievements of the skilful artillery-officer prove that in their applications to terrestrial motions these principles yield previsions of considerable exactness. But now, taking Mechanics as the type of a highly-developed science, let us note what it enables us to predict, and what it does not enable us to predict, respecting some concrete phenomenon. Say that there is a mine to be exploded. Ask what will happen to the fragments of matter sent into the air. Then observe how much we can infer from established dynamical laws. By that common observation which precedes the more exact observations of science, we are taught that all the fragments, having risen to heights more or less various, will fall; that they will reach the ground at scattered places within a circumscribed area, and at somewhat different times. Science enables us to say more than this. From those same principles whence are inferable the path of a planet or a projectile, it deduces the truth that each fragment will describe a curve; that all the curves, though individually different, will be specifically alike; that (ignoring deviations caused by atmospheric resistance) they will severally be portions of ellipses so eccentric as to be indistinguishable from parabolas—such parts of them, at least, as are described after the rush of gases ceases further to accelerate the fragments. But while the principles of Mechanics help us to these certainties, we cannot learn from them anything more definite respecting the courses that will be taken by particular fragments. Whether, of the mass overlying the powder to be exploded, the part on the left will be propelled upwards in one fragment or several? whether this piece will be shot higher than that? whether any, and if so, which, of the projected masses will be stopped in their courses by adjacent objects they strike?—are questions it cannot answer. *Not that there will be any want of conformity to law in these results*; but that the data on which predictions of them are to be based, cannot be obtained.

Observe, then, that respecting a concrete phenomenon of some complexity, the most exact science enables us to make predictions that are mainly general, or only partially special. Seeing that this is so, even where the causes and effects are not greatly involved, and where the science of them is well developed, much more may we expect it to be so among the most involved causes and effects, the science of which is but rudimentary. This contrast between the generalities that admit of prevision and the specialities that do not admit of prevision, will be still more clearly seen on passing from this preliminary illustration to an illustration in which the analogy is closer.

What can we say about the future of this newly-born child? Will it die of some disorder during infancy? Will it survive awhile, and be carried off by scarlet fever or whooping-cough? Will it have measles or small-pox, and succumb to one or the other? None of these questions can be answered. Will it some day fall down-stairs, or be run over, or set fire to its clothes; and be killed or maimed by one or other of these accidents? These questions also have no answers. None can tell whether in boyhood there may come epilepsy, or St. Vitus's dance, or other formidable affection. Looking at the child now in the nurse's arms, none can foresee with certainty that it will be stupid or intelligent, tractable or perverse. Equally beyond possibility of prediction are those events which, if it survives, will occur to it in maturity—partly caused by its own nature, and partly by surrounding conditions. Whether there will come the success due to skill and perseverance; whether the circumstances will be such as to give these scope or not; whether accidents will thwart or favour efforts; are wholly-unanswerable inquiries. That is to say, the facts we ordinarily class as biographical, do not admit of prevision.

If from quite special facts we turn to facts somewhat less special which the life of this infant will present, we find, among those that are *quasi*-biographical, a certain degree of prevision possible. Though the unfolding of the faculties is variable within limits, going on here precociously and there with unusual slowness, yet there is such order in the unfolding as enables us to say that the child will not be a mathematician or a dramatist at three years old, will not be a psychologist by the time he is ten, will not reach extended political conceptions while his voice is still unbroken. Moreover, of the emotional nature we may make certain predictions of a kindred order. Whether he will marry or not, no one can say; but it is possible to say, if not with certainty still with much probability, that after a certain age an inclination to marry will arise; and though none can tell whether he will have children, yet that, if he has, some amount of the paternal feeling will be manifested, may be concluded as very likely.

But now if, looking at the entire assemblage of facts that will be presented during the life of this infant as it becomes mature, decays, and dies, we pass over the biographical and *quasi*-biographical, as admitting of either no prevision or but imperfect prevision; we find remaining classes of facts that may be asserted beforehand: some with a high degree of probability, and some with certainty—some with great definiteness and some within moderate limits of variation. I refer to the facts of growth, development, structure, and function.

Along with that love of personalities which exalts everything inconstant in human life into a matter of interest, there goes the habit of regarding whatever is constant in human life as a matter of no interest; and so, when contemplating the future of the infant, there is a tacit ignoring of all the vital phenomena it will exhibit—phenomena that are alike knowable and important to be known. The anatomy and physiology of Man, comprehending under these names not only the structures and functions of the adult, but the progressive establishment of these structures and functions during individual evolution, form the subject-matter of what every one recognizes as a science. Though there is imperfect exactness in the generalized coexistences and sequences making up this science; though general truths respecting structures are met by occasional exceptions in the way of malformations; though anomalies of function also occur to negative absolute prediction; though there are considerable variations of the limits within which growth and structure may range, and considerable differences between the rates of functions and between the times at which functions are established; yet no one doubts that the biological phenomena presented by the human body, may be organized into a knowledge having the definiteness which constitutes it scientific, in the understood sense of that word.

If, now, any one, insisting on the incalculableness of a child's future, biographically considered, asserted that the child, therefore, presented no subject-matter for science, ignoring altogether what we will for the moment call its anthropology (though the meaning now given to the word scarcely permits this use of it), he would fall into a conspicuous error—an error in this case made conspicuous because we are able daily to observe the difference between an account of the living body, and an account of its conduct and the events that occur to it.

The reader doubtless anticipates the analogy. What Biography is to Anthropology, History is to Sociology—History, I mean, as commonly conceived. The kind of relation which the sayings and doings that make up the ordinary account of a man's life, bear to an account of his bodily and mental evolution, structural and functional, is like the kind of relation borne by that narrative of a nation's actions and fortunes its historian gives us, to a description of its institutions, regulative and operative, and the ways in which their structures and functions have gradually established themselves. And if it is an error to say that there is no Science of Man, because the events of a man's life cannot be foreseen, it is equally an error to say that there is no Science of Society, because there can be no prevision of the occurrences which make up ordinary history.

Of course, I do not say that the parallel between an individual organism and a social organism is so close, that the distinction to be clearly drawn in the one case may be drawn with like clearness in the other. The structures and functions of the social organism are obviously far less specific, far more modifiable, far more dependent on conditions that are variable and never twice alike. All I mean is that, as in the one case so in the other, there lie underneath the phenomena of conduct, not forming subject-matter for science, certain vital phenomena, which do form subject-matter for science. Just as in the man there are structures and functions which make possible the doings his biographer tells of, so in the nation there are structures and functions which make possible the doings its historian tells of; and in both cases it is with these structures and functions, in their origin, development, and decline, that science is concerned.

To make better the parallel, and further to explain the nature of the Social Science, we must say that the morphology and physiology of Society, instead of corresponding to the morphology and physiology of Man, correspond rather to morphology and physiology in general. Social organisms, like individual organisms, are to be arranged into classes and sub-classes—not, indeed, into classes and sub-classes having anything like the same definiteness or the same constancy, but nevertheless having likenesses and differences which justify the putting of them into major groups most-markedly contrasted, and, within these, arranging them in minor groups less-markedly contrasted. And just as Biology discovers certain general traits of development, structure, and function, holding throughout all organisms, others holding throughout certain great groups, others throughout certain sub-groups these contain; so Sociology has to recognize truths of social development, structure, and function, that are some of them universal, some of them general, some of them special.

For, recalling the conclusion previously reached, it is manifest that in so far as human beings, considered as social units, have properties in common, the social aggregates they form will have properties in common; that likenesses of nature holding throughout certain of the human races, will originate likenesses of nature in the nations arising out of them; and that such peculiar traits as are possessed by the highest varieties of men, must result in distinctive characters possessed in common by the communities into which they organize themselves.

So that whether we look at the matter in the abstract or in the concrete, we reach the same conclusion. We need but to glance, on the one hand, at the varieties of uncivilized men and the structures of their tribes, and, on the other hand, at the varieties of civilized men and the structures of their nations, to see inference verified by fact. And thus recognizing, both *à priori* and *à posteriori,* these relations between the phenomena of individual human nature and the phenomena of incorporated human nature, we cannot fail to see that the phenomena of incorporated human nature form the subject-matter of a science.

And now to make more definite the conception of a Social Science thus shadowed forth in a general way, let me set down a few truths of the kind indicated. Some that I propose to name are very familiar; and others I add, not because of their interest or importance, but because they are easy of exposition. The aim is simply to convey a clear idea of the nature of sociological truths.

Take, first, the general fact that along with social aggregation there always goes some kind of organization. In the very lowest stages, where the assemblages are very small and very incoherent, there is no established subordination—no centre of control. Chieftainships of settled kinds come only along with larger and more coherent aggregates. The evolution of a governmental structure having some strength and permanence, is the condition under which alone any considerable growth of a society can take place. A differentiation of the originally-homogeneous mass of units into a co-ordinating part and a co-ordinated part, is the indispensable initial step.

Along with evolution of societies in size there goes evolution of their co-ordinating centres; which, having become permanent, presently become more or less complex. In small tribes, chieftainship, generally wanting in stability, is quite simple; but as tribes become larger by growth, or by reduction of other tribes to subjection, the co-ordinating apparatus begins to develop by the addition of subordinate governing agencies.

Simple and familiar as are these facts, we are not, therefore, to overlook their significance. That men rise into the state of social aggregation only on condition that they lapse into relations of inequality in respect of power, and are made to co-operate as a whole only by the agency of a structure securing obedience, is none the less a fact in science because it is a trite fact. This is a primary common trait in social aggregates derived from a common trait in their units. It is a truth in Sociology, comparable to the biological truth that the first step in the production of any living organism, high or low, is a certain differentiation whereby a peripheral portion becomes distinguished from a central portion. And such exceptions to this biological truth as we find in those minute non-nucleated portions of protoplasm that are the very lowest living things, are paralleled by those exceptions to the sociological truth, seen in the small incoherent assemblages formed by the very lowest types of men.

The differentiation of the regulating part and the regulated part is, in small primitive societies, not only imperfectly established but vague. The chief does not at first become unlike his fellow-savages in his functions, otherwise than by exercising greater sway. He hunts, makes his weapons, works, and manages his private affairs, in just the same ways as the rest; while in war he differs from other warriors only by his predominant influence, not by ceasing to be a private soldier. And along with this slight separation from the rest of the tribe in military functions and industrial functions, there is only a slight separation politically: judicial action is but very feebly represented by exercise of his personal authority in keeping order.

At a higher stage, the power of the chief being well established, he no longer supports himself. Still he remains undistinguished industrially from other members of the dominant class, which has grown up while chieftainship has been getting settled; for he simply gets productive work done by deputy, as they do. Nor is a further extension of his power accompanied by complete separation of the political from the industrial functions; for he habitually remains a regulator of production, and in many cases a regulator of trade, presiding over acts of exchange. Of his several controlling activities, this last is, however, the one which he first ceases personally to carry on. Industry early shows a tendency towards self-control, apart from the control which the chief exercises more and more as political and military head. The primary social differentiation which we have noted between the regulative part and the operative part, is presently followed by a distinction, which eventually becomes very marked, between the internal arrangements of the two parts: the operative part slowly developing within itself agencies by which processes of production, distribution, and exchange are co-ordinated, while co-ordination of the non-operative part continues on its original footing.

Along with a development which renders conspicuous the separation of the operative and regulative structures, there goes a development within the regulative structures themselves. The chief, at first uniting the characters of king, judge, captain, and often priest, has his functions more and more specialized as the evolution of the society in size and complexity advances. Though remaining supreme judge, he does most of his judging by deputy; though remaining nominally head of his army, the actual leading of it falls more and more into the hands of subordinate officers; though still retaining ecclesiastical supremacy, his priestly functions practically almost cease; though in theory the maker and administrator of the law, the actual making and administration lapse more and more into other hands. So that, stating the facts broadly, out of the original co-ordinating agent having undivided functions, there eventually develop several co-ordinating agencies which divide these functions among them.

Each of these agencies, too, follows the same law. Originally simple, it step by step subdivides into many parts, and becomes an organization, administrative, judicial, ecclesiastical, or military, having graduated classes within itself, and a more or less distinct form of government within itself.

I will not complicate this statement by doing more than recognizing the variations that occur in cases where supreme power does not lapse into the hands of one man (which, however, in early stages of social evolution is an unstable modification). And I must explain that the above general statements are to be taken with the qualification that differences of detail are passed over to gain brevity and clearness. Add to which that it is beside the purpose of the argument to carry the description beyond these first stages. But duly bearing in mind that without here elaborating a Science of Sociology, nothing more than a rude outline of cardinal facts can be given, enough has been said to show that in the development of social structures, there may be recognized certain most-general facts, certain less-general facts, and certain facts successively more special; just as there may be recognized general and special facts of evolution in individual organisms.

To extend, as well as to make clearer, this conception of the Social Science, let me here set down a question which comes within its sphere. What is the relation in a society between structure and growth? Up to what point is structure necessary to growth? after what point does it retard growth? at what point does it arrest growth?

There exists in the individual organism a duplex relation between growth and structure which it is difficult adequately to express. Excluding the cases of a few low organisms living under special conditions, we may properly say that great growth is not possible without high structure. The whole animal kingdom, throughout its invertebrate and vertebrate types, may be cited in evidence. On the other hand, among the superior organisms, and especially among those leading active lives, there is a marked tendency for completion of structure to go along with arrest of growth. While an animal of elevated type is growing rapidly, its organs continue imperfectly developed—the bones remain partially cartilaginous, the muscles are soft, the brain lacks definiteness; and the details of structure throughout all parts are finished only after growth has ceased. Why these relations are as we find them, it is not difficult to see. That a young animal may grow, it must digest, circulate blood, breathe, excrete waste products, and so forth; to do which it must have tolerably-complete viscera, vascular system, etc. That it may eventually become able to get its own food, it has to develop gradually the needful appliances and aptitudes; to which end it must begin with limbs, and senses, and nervous system, that have considerable degrees of efficiency. But along with every increment of growth achieved by the help of these partially-developed structures, there has to go an alteration of the structures themselves. If they were rightly adjusted to the preceding smaller size, they are wrongly adjusted to the succeeding greater size. Hence they must be re-moulded—un-built and re-built. Manifestly, therefore, in proportion as the previous building has been complete, there arises a great obstacle in the shape of un-building and re-building. The bones show as how this difficulty is met. In the thigh-bone of a boy, for instance, there exists between the head and the cylindrical part of the bone, a place where the original cartilaginous state continues; and where, by the addition of new cartilage in which new osseous matter is deposited, the shaft of the bone is lengthened: the like going on in an answering place at the other end of the shaft. Complete ossification at these two places occurs only when the bone has ceased to increase in length; and, on considering what would have happened had the bone been ossified from end to end before its lengthening was complete, it will be seen how great an obstacle to growth is thus escaped. What holds here, holds throughout the organism: though structure up to a certain point is requisite for growth, structure beyond that point impedes growth. How necessary is this relation we shall equally perceive in a more complex case—say, the growth of an entire limb. There is a certain size and proportion of parts, which a limb ordinarily has in relation to the rest of the body. Throw upon that limb extra function, and within moderate limits it will increase in strength and bulk. If the extra function begins early in life, the limb may be raised considerably above its usual size; but if the extra function begins after maturity, the deviation is less: in neither case, however, being great. If we consider how increase of the limb is effected, we shall see why this is so. More active function brings a greater local supply of blood; and, for a time, new tissue is formed in excess of waste. But the local supply of blood is limited by the sizes of the arteries which bring it; and though, up to a certain point, increase of flow is gained by temporary dilatation of them, yet beyond that point increase can be gained only by un-building and re-building the arteries. Such alterations of arteries slowly take place—less slowly with the smaller peripheral ones, more slowly with the larger ones out of which these branch; since these have to be altered all the way back to their points of divergence from the great central blood vessels. In like manner, the channels for carrying off waste products must be re-modelled, both locally and centrally. The nerve-trunks, too, and also the centres from which they come, must be adjusted to the greater demands upon them. Nay, more; with a given visceral system, a large extra quantity of blood cannot be permanently given to one part of the body, without decreasing the quantities given to other parts; and, therefore, structural changes have to be made by which the drafting-off of blood to these other parts is diminished. Hence the great resistance to increase in the size of a limb beyond a certain moderate limit. Such increase cannot be effected without un-building and re-building not only the parts that directly minister to the limb, but, eventually, all the remoter parts. So that the bringing of structures into perfect fitness for certain requirements, immensely hinders the adaptation of them to other requirements—re-adjustments become difficult in proportion as adjustments are made complete.

How far does this law hold in the social organism? To what extent does it happen here, too, that the multiplying and elaborating of institutions, and the perfecting of arrangements for gaining immediate ends, raise impediments to the development of better institutions and to the future gaining of higher ends? Socially, as well as individually, organization is indispensable to growth: beyond a certain point there cannot be further growth, without further organization. Yet there is not a little reason for suspecting that beyond this point organization is indirectly repressive—increases the obstacles to those re-adjustments required for larger growth and more perfect structure. Doubtless the aggregate we call a society is much more plastic than an individual living aggregate to which it is here compared—its type is far less fixed. Nevertheless, there is evidence that its type tends continually to become fixed, and that each addition to its structures is a step towards the fixation.

William Graham Sumner

1840-1910

Source: *Folkways: A Study of the Sociological Importance of Usage, Manners, Customs, Mores, and Morals* (1906)
Selection: Chapter I: Fundamental Notions of Folkways and Mores, pp. 1-31

Sumner grew up in Massachusetts, graduated from Yale College in 1863, and was an Episcopal minister early in his career. In 1875 he became the first academician to teach a course entitled "sociology" in the English-speaking world, at Yale, which focused on the thought of Comte and Spencer. In general, Sumner brought a conservative perspective to the new science of sociology, including his ideas about the economic survival of the fittest, following Spencer and other "Social Darwinists" of the time. He also wrote popular essays for a wide audience that supported his advocacy of free markets, anti-imperialism, and the gold standard. Despite his conservative political bent and once having been an Episcopal minister, Sumner was instrumental in modernizing the American university system away from its old "divinity-classics" roots. His most well known book is Folkways, *published in 1906, two years before he began his one-year tenure as president of the American Sociological Association. In the writing below from* Folkways, *Sumner defines and elaborates on the concepts of folkways and mores while also exhibiting his Social Darwinist perspective in analyzing societies.*

*

Definition and Mode of Origin of the Folkways. If we put together all that we have learned from anthropology and ethnography about primitive men and primitive society, we perceive that the first task of life is to live. Men begin with acts, not with thoughts. Every moment brings necessities which must be satisfied at once. Need was the first experience, and it was followed at once by a blundering effort to satisfy it. It is generally taken for granted that men inherited some guiding instincts from their beast ancestry, and it may be true, although it has never been proved. If there were such inheritances, they controlled and aided the first efforts to satisfy needs. Analogy makes it easy to assume that the ways of beasts had produced channels of habit and predisposition along which dexterities and other psychophysical activities would run easily. Experiments with newborn animals show that in the absence of any experience of the relation of means to ends, efforts to satisfy needs are clumsy and blundering.

The method is that of trial and failure, which produces repeated pain, loss, and disappointments. Nevertheless, it is a method of rude experiment and selection. The earliest efforts of men were of this kind. Need was the impelling force. Pleasure and pain, on the one side and the other, were the rude constraints which defined the line on which efforts must proceed. The ability to distinguish between pleasure and pain is the only psychical power which is to be assumed. Thus ways of doing things were selected, which were expedient. They answered the purpose better than other ways, or with less toil and pain. Along the course on which efforts were compelled to go, habit, routine, and skill were developed. The struggle to maintain existence was carried on, not individually, but in groups. Each profited by the other's experience; hence there was concurrence towards that which proved to be most expedient. All at last adopted the same way for the same purpose; hence the ways turned into customs and became mass phenomena. Instincts were developed in connection with them. In this way folkways arise. The young learn them by tradition, imitation, and authority. The folkways, at a time, provide for all the needs of life then and there. They are uniform, universal in the group, imperative, and invariable. As time goes on, the folkways become more and more arbitrary, positive, and imperative. If asked why they act in a certain way in certain cases, primitive people always answer that it is because they and their ancestors always have done so. A sanction also arises from ghost fear. The ghosts of ancestors would be angry if the living should change the ancient folkways.

The Folkways Are a Societal force. The operation by which folkways are produced consists in the frequent repetition of petty acts, often by great numbers acting in concert or, at least, acting the same way when face to face with the same need. The immediate motive is interest. It produces habit in the individual and custom in the group. It is, therefore, in the highest degree original and primitive. By habit and custom it exerts a strain on every individual within its range; therefore it rises to a societal force to which great classes of societal phenomena are due. Its earliest stages, its course, and laws may be studied; also its influence on individuals and their reaction on it. It is our purpose to study it. We have to recognize it as one of the chief forces by which a society is made to be what it is. Out of the unconscious experiment which every repetition of the ways includes, there issues pleasure or pain, and then, so far as the men are capable of reflection, convictions that the ways are conducive to societal welfare. These two experiences are not the same. The most uncivilized men, both in the food quest and in war, do things which are painful, but which have been found to be expedient. Perhaps these cases teach the sense of social welfare better than those which are pleasurable and favorable to welfare. The former cases call for intelligent reflection on experience. When this conviction as to the relation to welfare is added to the folkways they are converted into mores, and, by virtue of the philosophical and ethical element added to them, they win utility and importance and become the source of the science and the art of living.

Folkways Are Made Unconsciously. It is of the first importance to notice that, from the first acts by which men try to satisfy needs, each act stands by itself, and looks no further than the immediate satisfaction. From recurrent needs arise habits for the individual and customs for the group, but these results are consequences which were never conscious, and never foreseen or intended. They are not noticed until they have long existed, and it is still longer before they are appreciated. Another long time must pass, and a higher stage of mental development must be reached, before they can be used as a basis from which to deduce rules for meeting, in the future, problems whose pressure can be foreseen. The folkways, therefore, are not creations of human purpose and wit. They are like products of natural forces which men unconsciously set in operation, or they are like the instinctive ways of animals, which are developed out of experience, which reach a final form of maximum adaptation to an interest, which are handed down by tradition and admit of no exception or variation, yet change to meet new conditions, still within the same limited methods, and without rational reflection or purpose. From this it results that all the life of human beings, in all ages and stages of culture, is primarily controlled by a vast mass of folkways handed down from the earliest existence of the race, having the nature of the ways of other animals, only the topmost layers of which are subject to change and control, and have been somewhat modified by human philosophy, ethics, and religion, or by other acts of intelligent reflection. We are told of savages that "It is difficult to exhaust the customs and small ceremonial usages of a savage people. Custom regulates the whole of a man's actions,—his bathing, washing, cutting his hair, eating, drinking, and fasting. From his cradle to his grave he is the slave of ancient usage. In his life there is nothing free, nothing original, nothing spontaneous, no progress towards a higher and better life, and no attempt to improve his condition, mentally, morally, or spiritually." All men act in this way with only a little wider margin of voluntary variation. [. . .]

The Strain of Improvement and Consistency. The folkways, being ways of satisfying needs, have succeeded more or less well, and therefore have produced more or less pleasure or pain. Their quality always consisted in their adaptation to the purpose. If they were imperfectly adapted and unsuccessful, they produced pain, which drove men on to learn better. The folkways are, therefore, (1) subject to a strain of improvement towards better adaptation of means to ends, as long as the adaptation is so imperfect that pain is produced. They are also (2) subject to a strain of consistency with each other, because they all answer their several purposes with less friction and antagonism when they cooperate and support each other. The forms of industry, the forms of the family, the notions of property, the constructions of rights, and the types of religion show the strain of consistency with each other through the whole history of civilization. The two great cultural divisions of the human race are the oriental and the occidental. Each is consistent throughout; each has its own philosophy and spirit; they are separated from top to bottom by different mores, different standpoints, different ways, and different notions of what societal arrangements are advantageous. In their contrast they keep before our minds the possible range of divergence in the solution of the great problems of human life, and in the views of earthly existence by which life policy may be controlled. If two planets were joined in one, their inhabitants could not differ more widely as to what things are best worth seeking, or what ways are most expedient for well living.

The Aleatory Interest. If we should try to find a specimen society in which expedient ways of satisfying needs and interests were found by trial and failure, and by long selection from experience, as broadly described in sec. i above, it might be impossible to find one. Such a practical and utilitarian mode of procedure, even when mixed with ghost sanction, is rationalistic. It would not be suited to the ways and temper of primitive men. There was an element in the most elementary experience which was irrational and defied all expedient methods. One might use the best known means with the greatest care, yet fail of the result. On the other hand, one might get a great result with no effort at all. One might also incur a calamity without any fault of his own. This was the aleatory element in life, the element of risk and loss, good or bad fortune. This element is never absent from the affairs of men. It has greatly influenced their life philosophy and policy. On one side, good luck may mean something for nothing, the extreme case of prosperity and felicity. On the other side, ill luck may mean failure, loss, calamity, and disappointment, in spite of the most earnest and well-planned endeavor. The minds of men always dwell more on bad luck. They accept ordinary prosperity as a matter of course. Misfortunes arrest their attention and remain in their memory. Hence the ills of life are the mode of manifestation of the aleatory element which has most affected life policy. Primitive men ascribed all incidents to the agency of men or of ghosts and spirits. Good and ill luck were attributed to the superior powers; and were supposed to be due to their pleasure or displeasure at the conduct of men. This group of notions constitutes goblinism. It furnishes a complete world philosophy. The element of luck is always present in the struggle for existence. That is why primitive men never could carry on the struggle for existence, disregarding the aleatory element and employing a utilitarian method only. The aleatory element has always been the connecting link between the struggle for existence and religion. It was only by religious rites that the aleatory element in the struggle for existence could be controlled. The notions of ghosts, demons, another world, etc., were all fantastic. They lacked all connection with facts, and were arbitrary constructions put upon experience. They were poetic and developed by poetic construction and imaginative deduction. The nexus between them and events was not cause and effect, but magic. They therefore led to delusive deductions in regard to life and its meaning, which entered into subsequent action as guiding faiths, and imperative notions about the conditions of success. The authority of religion and that of custom coalesced into one indivisible obligation. Therefore the simple statement of experiment and expediency in the first paragraph above is not derived directly from actual cases, but is a product of analysis and inference. It must also be added that vanity and ghost fear produced needs which man was as eager to satisfy as those of hunger of the family. Folkways resulted for the former as well as for the latter.

All Origins Are Lost in Mystery. No objection can lie against this postulate about the way in which folkways began, on account of the element of inference in it. All origins are lost in mystery, and it seems vain to hope that from any origin the veil of mystery will ever be raised. We go up the stream of history to the utmost point for which we have evidence of its course. Then we are forced to reach out into the darkness upon the line of direction marked by the remotest course of the historic stream. This is the way in which we have to act in regard to the origin of capital, language, the family, the state, religion, and rights. We never can hope to see the beginning of any one of these things. Use and wont are products and results. They had antecedents. We never can find or see the first member of the series. It is only by analysis and inference that we can form any conception of the "beginning" which we are always so eager to find. [. . .]

The Struggle for Existence and the Competition of Life; Antagonistic Cooperation. The struggle for existence must be carried on under life conditions and in connection with the competition of life. The life conditions consist in variable elements of the environment, the supply of materials necessary to support life, the difficulty of exploiting them, the state of the arts, and the circumstances of physiography, climate, meteorology, etc., which favor life or the contrary. The struggle for existence is a process in which an individual and nature are the parties. The individual is engaged in a process by which he wins from his environment what he needs to support his existence. In the competition of life the parties are men and other organisms. The men strive with each other, or with the flora and fauna with which they are associated. The competition of life is the rivalry, antagonism, and mutual displacement in which the individual is involved with other organisms by his efforts to carry on the struggle for existence for himself. It is, therefore, the competition of life which is the societal element, and which produces societal organization. The number present and in competition is another of the life conditions. At a time and place the life conditions are the same for a number of human beings who are present, and the problems of life policy are the same. This is another reason why the attempts to satisfy interest become mass phenomena and result in folkways. The individual and social elements are always in interplay with each other if there are a number present. If one is trying to carry on the struggle for existence with nature, the fact that others are doing the same in the same environment is an essential condition for him. Then arises an alternative. He and the others may so interfere with each other that all shall fail, or they may combine, and by cooperation raise their efforts against nature to a higher power. This latter method is industrial organization. The crisis which produces it is constantly renewed, and men are forced to raise the organization to greater complexity and more comprehensive power, without limit. Interests are the relations of action and reaction between the individual and the life conditions, through which relations the evolution of the individual is produced. That evolution, so long as it goes on prosperously, is well living, and it results in the self-realization of the individual, for we may think of each one as capable of fulfilling some career and attaining to some character and state of power by the developing of predispositions which he possesses. It would be an error, however, to suppose that all nature is a chaos of warfare and competition. Combination and cooperation are so fundamentally necessary that even very low life forms are found in symbiosis for mutual dependence and assistance. A combination can exist where each of its members would perish. Competition and combination are two forms of life association which alternate through the whole organic and superorganic domains. The neglect of this fact leads to many socialistic fallacies. Combination is of the essence of organization, and organization is the great device for increased power by a number of unequal and dissimilar units brought into association for a common purpose. [. . .]

The Folkways Are "Right." Rights. Morals. The folkways are the "right" ways to satisfy all interests, because they are traditional, and exist in fact. They extend over the whole of life. There is a right way to catch game, to win a wife, to make one's self appear, to cure disease, to honor ghosts, to treat comrades or strangers, to behave when a child is born, on the warpath, in council, and so on in all cases which can arise. The ways are defined on the negative side, that is, by taboos. The "right" way is the way which the ancestors used and which has been handed down. The tradition is its own warrant. It is not held subject to verification by experience. The notion of right is in the folkways. It is not outside of them, of independent origin, and brought to them to test them. In the folkways, whatever is, is right. This is because they are traditional, and therefore contain in themselves the authority of the ancestral ghosts. When we come to the folkways we are at the end of our analysis. The notion of right and ought is the same in regard to all the folkways, but the degree of it varies with the importance of the interest at stake. The obligation of conformable and cooperative action is far greater under ghost fear and war than in other matters, and the social sanctions are severer, because group interests are supposed to be at stake. Some usages contain only a slight element of right and ought. It may well be believed that notions of right and duty, and of social welfare, were first developed in connection with ghost fear and other-worldliness, and therefore that, in that field also, folkways were first raised to mores. "Rights" are the rules of mutual give and take in the competition of life which are imposed on comrades in the in-group, in order that the peace may prevail there which is essential to the group strength. Therefore rights can never be "natural" or "God-given," or absolute in any sense. The morality of a group at a time is the sum of the taboos and prescriptions in the folkways by which right conduct is defined. Therefore morals can never be intuitive. They are historical, institutional, and empirical.

World philosophy, life policy, right, rights, and morality are all products of the folkways. They are reflections on, and generalizations from, the experience of pleasure and pain which is won in efforts to carry on the struggle for existence under actual life conditions. The generalizations are very crude and vague in their germinal forms. They are all embodied in folklore, and all our philosophy and science have been developed out of them.

The Folkways Are "True." the folkways are necessarily "true" with respect to some world philosophy. Pain forced men to think. The ills of life imposed reflection and taught forethought. Mental processes were irksome and were not undertaken until painful experience made them unavoidable. With great unanimity all over the globe primitive men followed the same line of thought. The dead were believed to live on as ghosts in another world just like this one. The ghosts had just the same needs, tastes, passions, etc., as the living men had had. These transcendental notions were the beginning of the mental outfit of mankind. They are articles of faith, not rational convictions. The living had duties to the ghosts, and the ghosts had rights; they also had power to enforce their rights. It behooved the living therefore to learn how to deal with ghosts. Here we have a complete world philosophy and a life policy deduced from it. When pain, loss, and ill were experienced and the question was provoked, Who did this to us? the world philosophy furnished the answer. When the painful experience forced the question, Why are the ghosts angry and what must we do to appease them? the "right" answer was the one which fitted into the philosophy of ghost fear. All acts were therefore constrained and trained into the forms of the world philosophy by ghost fear, ancestral authority, taboos, and habit. The habits and customs created a practical philosophy of welfare, and they confirmed and developed the religious theories of goblinism. [. . .]

Definition of the Mores. When the elements of truth and right are developed into doctrines of welfare, the folkways are raised to another plane. They then become capable of producing inferences, developing into new forms, and extending their constructive influence over men and society. Then we call them the mores. The mores are the folkways, including the philosophical and ethical generalizations as to societal welfare which are suggested by them, and inherent in them, as they grow.

Taboos. The mores necessarily consist, in a large part, of taboos, which indicate the things which must not be done. In part these are dictated by mystic dread of ghosts who might be offended by certain acts, but they also include such acts as have been found by experience to produce unwelcome results, especially in the food quest, in war, in health, or in increase or decrease of population. These taboos always contain a greater element of philosophy than the positive rules, because the taboos contain reference to a reason, as, for instance, that the act would displease the ghosts. The primitive taboos correspond to the fact that the life of man is environed by perils. His food quest must be limited by shunning poisonous plants. His appetite must be restrained from excess. His physical strength and health must be guarded from dangers. The taboos carry on the accumulated wisdom of generations, which has almost always been purchased by pain, loss, disease, and death. Other taboos contain inhibitions of what will be injurious to the group. The laws about the sexes, about property, about war, and about ghosts have this character. They always include some social philosophy. They are both mystic and utilitarian, or compounded of the two.

Taboos may be divided into two classes, (1) protective and (2) destructive. Some of them aim to protect and secure, while others aim to repress or exterminate. Women are subject to some taboos which are directed against them as sources of possible harm or danger to men, and they are subject to other taboos which put them outside of the duties or risks of men. On account of this difference in taboos, taboos act selectively, and thus affect the course of civilization. They contain judgments as to societal welfare.

GUSTAVE LE BON

1841-1931

Source: *The Crowd: A Study of the Popular Mind* (1896 edition)

Selection: Introduction: The Era of Crowds, pp. xiii-xxiv, and Book I, Chapter I: General Characteristics of Crowds, pp. 1-15

A French sociologist, social psychologist, and amateur physicist, Le Bon was the author of several works that expounded theories of national traits, racial superiority, herd behavior and crowd psychology. Before becoming a social theorist he received a doctorate of medicine, and his interests eventually shifted to natural science and social psychology. In The Psychology of Peoples (1894) *he developed a view that history is the product of racial or national character, with emotion, not intelligence, the dominant force in social evolution. He attributed true progress to the work of intellectual elites, but believed modern life was increasingly characterized by crowd assemblages and the psychology of crowds. Thus his work was often used by politicians and media researchers throughout the early decades of the twentieth century. In the writings below from his most popular work,* The Crowd, *one can clearly see the basis of his reasoning that crowd behavior is emotional and intellectually weak, and that the conscious personality of the individual in a crowd becomes subordinate to the dominant crowd mind.*

*

The Era of Crowds. The great upheavals which precede changes of civilisations such as the fall of the Roman Empire and the foundation of the Arabian Empire, seem at first sight determined more especially by political transformations, foreign invasion, or the overthrow of dynasties. But a more attentive study of these events shows that behind their apparent causes the real cause is generally seen to be a profound modification in the ideas of the peoples. The true historical upheavals are not those which astonish us by their grandeur and violence. The only important changes from which the renewal of civilisations results affect ideas, conceptions, and beliefs. The memorable events of history are the visible effects of the invisible changes of human thought. The reason these great events are rare is that there is nothing so stable in a race as the inherited groundwork of its thoughts.

The present epoch is one of these critical moments in which the thought of mankind is undergoing a process of transformation.

Two fundamental factors are at the base of this transformation. The first is the destruction of those religious, political, and social beliefs in which all the elements of our civilisation are rooted. The second is the creation of entirely new conditions of existence and thought as the result of modern scientific and industrial discoveries.

The ideas of the past, although half destroyed, being still very powerful, and the ideas which are to replace them being still in process of formation, the modern age represents a period of transition and anarchy.

It is not easy to say as yet what will one day be evolved from this necessarily somewhat chaotic period. What will be the fundamental ideas on which the societies that are to succeed our own will be built up? We do not at present know. Still it is already clear that on whatever lines the societies of the future are organised, they will have to count with a new power, with the last surviving sovereign force of modern times, the power of crowds. On the ruins of so many ideas formerly considered beyond discussion, and today decayed or decaying, of so many sources of authority that successive revolutions have destroyed, this power, which alone has arisen in their stead, seems soon destined to absorb the others. While all our ancient beliefs are tottering and disappearing, while the old pillars of society are giving way one by one, the power of the crowd is the only force that nothing menaces, and of which the prestige is continually on the increase. The age we are about to enter will in truth be the ERA OF CROWDS.

Scarcely a century ago the traditional policy of European states and the rivalries of sovereigns were the principal factors that shaped events. The opinion of the masses scarcely counted, and most frequently indeed did not count at all. Today it is the traditions which used to obtain in politics, and the individual tendencies and rivalries of rulers which do not count; while, on the contrary, the voice of the masses has become preponderant. It is this voice that dictates their conduct to kings, whose endeavour is to take note of its utterances. The destinies of nations are elaborated at present in the heart of the masses, and no longer in the councils of princes.

The entry of the popular classes into political life—that is to say, in reality, their progressive transformation into governing classes—is one of the most striking characteristics of our epoch of transition. The introduction of universal suffrage, which exercised for a long time but little influence, is not, as might be thought, the distinguishing feature of this transference of political power. The progressive growth of the power of the masses took place at first by the propagation of certain ideas, which have slowly implanted themselves in men's minds, and afterwards by the gradual association of individuals bent on bringing about the realisation of theoretical conceptions. It is by association that crowds have come to procure ideas with respect to their interests which are very clearly defined if not particularly just, and have arrived at a consciousness of their strength. The masses are founding syndicates before which the authorities capitulate one after the other; they are also founding labour unions, which in spite of all economic laws tend to regulate the conditions of labour and wages. They return to assemblies in which the Government is vested, representatives utterly lacking initiative and independence, and reduced most often to nothing else than the spokesmen of the committees that have chosen them.

Today the claims of the masses are becoming more and more sharply defined, and amount to nothing less than a determination to utterly destroy society as it now exists, with a view to making it hark back to that primitive communism which was the normal condition of all human groups before the dawn of civilisation. Limitations of the hours of labour, the nationalisation of mines, railways, factories, and the soil, the equal distribution of all products, the elimination of all the upper classes for the benefit of the popular classes, etc., such are these claims.

Little adapted to reasoning, crowds, on the contrary, are quick to act. As the result of their present organisation their strength has become immense. The dogmas whose birth we are witnessing will soon have the force of the old dogmas; that is to say, the tyrannical and sovereign force of being above discussion. The divine right of the masses is about to replace the divine right of kings.

The writers who enjoy the favour of our middle classes, those who best represent their rather narrow ideas, their somewhat prescribed views, their rather superficial scepticism, and their at times somewhat excessive egoism, display profound alarm at this new power which they see growing; and to combat the disorder in men's minds they are addressing despairing appeals to those moral forces of the Church for which they formerly professed so much disdain. They talk to us of the bankruptcy of science, go back in penitence to Rome, and remind us of the teachings of revealed truth. These new converts forget that it is too late. Had they been really touched by grace, a like operation could not have the same influence on minds less concerned with the preoccupations which beset these recent adherents to religion. The masses repudiate today the gods which their admonishers repudiated yesterday and helped to destroy. There is no power, Divine or human, that can oblige a stream to flow back to its source.

There has been no bankruptcy of science, and science has had no share in the present intellectual anarchy, nor in the making of the new power which is springing up in the midst of this anarchy. Science promised us truth, or at least a knowledge of such relations as our intelligence can seize: it never promised us peace or happiness. Sovereignly indifferent to our feelings, it is deaf to our lamentations. It is for us to endeavour to live with science, since nothing can bring back the illusions it has destroyed.

Universal symptoms, visible in all nations, show us the rapid growth of the power of crowds, and do not admit of our supposing that it is destined to cease growing at an early date. Whatever fate it may reserve for us, we shall have to submit to it. All reasoning against it is a mere vain war of words. Certainly it is possible that the advent to power of the masses marks one of the last stages of Western civilisation, a complete return to those periods of confused anarchy which seem always destined to precede the birth of every new society. But may this result be prevented?

Up to now these thoroughgoing destructions of a worn-out civilisation have constituted the most obvious task of the masses. It is not indeed today merely that this can be traced. History tells us, that from the moment when the moral forces on which a civilisation rested have lost their strength, its final dissolution is brought about by those unconscious and brutal crowds known, justifiably enough, as barbarians. Civilisations as yet have only been created and directed by a small intellectual aristocracy, never by crowds. Crowds are only powerful for destruction. Their rule is always tantamount to a barbarian phase. A civilisation involves fixed rules, discipline, a passing from the instinctive to the rational state, forethought for the future, an elevated degree of culture—all of them conditions that crowds, left to themselves, have invariably shown themselves incapable of realising. In consequence of the purely destructive nature of their power, crowds act like those microbes which hasten the dissolution of enfeebled or dead bodies. When the structure of a civilisation is rotten, it is always the masses that bring about its downfall. It is at such a juncture that their chief mission is plainly visible, and that for a while the philosophy of number seems the only philosophy of history.

Is the same fate in store for our civilisation? There is ground to fear that this is the case, but we are not as yet in a position to be certain of it.

However this may be, we are bound to resign ourselves to the reign of the masses, since want of foresight has in succession overthrown all the barriers that might have kept the crowd in check.

We have a very slight knowledge of these crowds which are beginning to be the object of so much discussion. Professional students of psychology, having lived far from them, have always ignored them, and when, as of late, they have turned their attention in this direction it has only been to consider the crimes crowds are capable of committing. Without a doubt criminal crowds exist, but virtuous and heroic crowds, and crowds of many other kinds, are also to be met with. The crimes of crowds only constitute a particular phase of their psychology. The mental constitution of crowds is not to be learnt merely by a study of their crimes, any more than that of an individual by a mere description of his vices.

However, in point of fact, all the world's masters, all the founders of religions or empires, the apostles of all beliefs, eminent statesmen, and, in a more modest sphere, the mere chiefs of small groups of men have always been unconscious psychologists, possessed of an instinctive and often very sure knowledge of the character of crowds, and it is their accurate knowledge of this character that has enabled them to so easily establish their mastery. Napoleon had a marvellous insight into the psychology of the masses of the country over which he reigned, but he, at times, completely misunderstood the psychology of crowds belonging to other races; and it is because he thus misunderstood it that he engaged in Spain, and notably in Russia, in conflicts in which his power received blows which were destined within a brief space of time to ruin it. A knowledge of the psychology of crowds is today the last resource of the statesman who wishes not to govern them—that is becoming a very difficult matter—but at any rate not to be too much governed by them.

His most subtle advisers, moreover, did not understand this psychology any better. Talleyrand wrote him that "Spain would receive his soldiers as liberators." It received them as beasts of prey. A psychologist acquainted with the hereditary instincts of the Spanish race would have easily foreseen this reception.

It is only by obtaining some sort of insight into the psychology of crowds that it can be understood how slight is the action upon them of laws and institutions, how powerless they are to hold any opinions other than those which are imposed upon them, and that it is not with rules based on theories of pure equity that they are to be led, but by seeking what produces an impression on them and what seduces them. For instance, should a legislator, wishing to impose a new tax, choose that which would be theoretically the most just? By no means. In practice the most unjust may be the best for the masses. Should it at the same time be the least obvious, and apparently the least burdensome, it will be the most easily tolerated. [. . .]

Many other practical applications might be made of the psychology of crowds. A knowledge of this science throws the most vivid light on a great number of historical and economic phenomena totally incomprehensible without it. I shall have occasion to show that the reason why the most remarkable of modern historians, Taine, has at times so imperfectly understood the events of the great French Revolution is, that it never occurred to him to study the genius of crowds. He took as his guide in the study of this complicated period the descriptive method resorted to by naturalists; but the moral forces are almost absent in the case of the phenomena which naturalists have to study. Yet it is precisely these forces that constitute the true mainsprings of history.

In consequence, merely looked at from its practical side, the study of the psychology of crowds deserved to be attempted. Were its interest that resulting from pure curiosity only, it would still merit attention. It is as interesting to decipher the motives of the actions of men as to determine the characteristics of a mineral or a plant. Our study of the genius of crowds can merely be a brief synthesis, a simple summary of our investigations. Nothing more must be demanded of it than a few suggestive views. Others will work the ground more thoroughly. Today we only touch the surface of a still almost virgin soil.

The Mind of Crowds: General Characteristics of Crowds. In its ordinary sense the word "crowd" means a gathering of individuals of whatever nationality, profession, or sex, and whatever be the chances that have brought them together. From the psychological point of view the expression "crowd" assumes quite a different signification. Under certain given circumstances, and only under those circumstances, an agglomeration of men presents new characteristics very different from those of the individuals composing it. The sentiments and ideas of all the persons in the gathering take one and the same direction, and their conscious personality vanishes. A collective mind is formed, doubtless transitory, but presenting very clearly defined characteristics. The gathering has thus become what, in the absence of a better expression, I will call an organised crowd, or, if the term is considered preferable, a psychological crowd. It forms a single being, and is subjected to the *law of the mental unity of crowds*.

It is evident that it is not by the mere fact of a number of individuals finding themselves accidentally side by side that they acquire the character of an organised crowd. A thousand individuals accidentally gathered in a public place without any determined object in no way constitute a crowd from the psychological point of view. To acquire the special characteristics of such a crowd, the influence is necessary of certain predisposing causes of which we shall have to determine the nature.

The disappearance of conscious personality and the turning of feelings and thoughts in a definite direction, which are the primary characterristics of a crowd about to become organised, do not always involve the simultaneous presence of a number of individuals on one spot. Thousands of isolated individuals may acquire at certain moments, and under the influence of certain violent emotions—such, for example, as a great national event—the characteristics of a psychological crowd. It will be sufficient in that case that a mere chance should bring them together for their acts to at once assume the characteristics peculiar to the acts of a crowd. At certain moments half a dozen men might constitute a psychological crowd, which may not happen in the case of hundreds of men gathered together by accident. On the other hand, an entire nation, though there may be no visible agglomeration, may become a crowd under the action of certain influences.

A psychological crowd once constituted, it acquires certain provisional but determinable general characteristics. To these general characteristics there are adjoined particular characteristics which vary according to the elements of which the crowd is composed, and may modify its mental constitution. Psychological crowds, then, are susceptible of classification; and when we come to occupy ourselves with this matter, we shall see that a heterogeneous crowd—that is, a crowd composed of dissimilar elements—presents certain characteristics in common with homogeneous crowds—that is, with crowds composed of elements more or less akin (sects, castes, and classes)—and side by side with these common characteristics particularities which permit of the two kinds of crowds being differentiated.

But before occupying ourselves with the different categories of crowds, we must first of all examine the characteristics common to them all. We shall set to work like the naturalist, who begins by describing the general characteristics common to all the members of a family before concerning himself with the particular characteristics which allow the differentiation of the genera and species that the family includes.

It is not easy to describe the mind of crowds with exactness, because its organisation varies not only according to race and composition, but also according to the nature and intensity of the exciting causes to which crowds are subjected. The same difficulty, however, presents itself in the psychological study of an individual. It is only in novels that individuals are found to traverse their whole life with an unvarying character. It is only the uniformity of the environment that creates the apparent uniformity of characters. I have shown elsewhere that all mental constitutions contain possibilities of character which may be manifested in consequence of a sudden change of environment. This explains how it was that among the most savage members of the French Convention were to be found inoffensive citizens who, under ordinary circumstances, would have been peaceable notaries or virtuous magistrates. The storm past, they resumed their normal character of quiet, law-abiding citizens. Napoleon found amongst them his most docile servants.

It being impossible to study here all the successive degrees of organisation of crowds, we shall concern ourselves more especially with such crowds as have attained to the phase of complete organisation. In this way we shall see what crowds may become, but not what they invariably are. It is only in this advanced phase of organisation that certain new and special characteristics are superposed on the unvarying and dominant character of the race; then takes place that turning already alluded to of all the feelings and thoughts of the collectivity in an identical direction. It is only under such circumstances, too, that what I have called above the *psychological law of the mental unity of crowds* comes into play.

Among the psychological characteristics of crowds there are some that they may present in common with isolated individuals, and others, on the contrary, which are absolutely peculiar to them and are only to be met with in collectivities. It is these special characteristics that we shall study, first of all, in order to show their importance.

The most striking peculiarity presented by a psychological crowd is the following: Whoever be the individuals that compose it, however like or unlike be their mode of life, their occupations, their character, or their intelligence, the fact that they have been transformed into a crowd puts them in possession of a sort of collective mind which makes them feel, think, and act in a manner quite different from that in which each individual of them would feel, think, and act were he in a state of isolation. There are certain ideas and feelings which do not come into being, or do not transform themselves into acts except in the case of individuals forming a crowd. The psychological crowd is a provisional being formed of heterogeneous elements, which for a moment are combined, exactly as the cells which constitute a living body form by their reunion a new being which displays characteristics very different from those possessed by each of the cells singly.

Contrary to an opinion which one is astonished to find coming from the pen of so acute a philosopher as Herbert Spencer, in the aggregate which constitutes a crowd there is in no sort a summing-up of or an average struck between its elements. What really takes place is a combination followed by the creation of new characteristics, just as in chemistry certain elements, when brought into contact—bases and acids, for example—combine to form a new body possessing properties quite different from those of the bodies that have served to form it.

It is easy to prove how much the individual forming part of a crowd differs from the isolated individual, but it is less easy to discover the causes of this difference.

To obtain at any rate a glimpse of them it is necessary in the first place to call to mind the truth established by modern psychology, that unconscious phenomena play an altogether preponderating part not only in organic life, but also in the operations of the intelligence. The conscious life of the mind is of small importance in comparison with its unconscious life. The most subtle analyst, the most acute observer, is scarcely successful in discovering more than a very small number of the unconscious motives that determine his conduct. Our conscious acts are the outcome of an unconscious substratum created in the mind in the main by hereditary influences. This substratum consists of the innumerable common characteristics handed down from generation to generation, which constitute the genius of a race. Behind the avowed causes of our acts there undoubtedly lie secret causes that we do not avow, but behind these secret causes there are many others more secret still which we ourselves ignore. The greater part of our daily actions are the result of hidden motives which escape our observation.

It is more especially with respect to those unconscious elements which constitute the genius of a race that all the individuals belonging to it resemble each other, while it is principally in respect to the conscious elements of their character—the fruit of education, and yet more of exceptional hereditary conditions—that they differ from each other. Men the most unlike in the matter of their intelligence possess instincts, passions, and feelings that are very similar. In the case of every thing that belongs to the realm of sentiment—religion, politics, morality, the affections and antipathies, etc.—the most eminent men seldom surpass the standard of the most ordinary individuals. From the intellectual point of view an abyss may exist between a great mathematician and his boot maker, but from the point of view of character the difference is most often slight or non-existent.

It is precisely these general qualities of character, governed by forces of which we are unconscious, and possessed by the majority of the normal individuals of a race in much the same degree—it is precisely these qualities, I say, that in crowds become common property. In the collective mind the intellectual aptitudes of the individuals, and in consequence their individuality, are weakened. The heterogeneous is swamped by the homogeneous, and the unconscious qualities obtain the upper hand.

This very fact that crowds possess in common ordinary qualities explains why they can never accomplish acts demanding a high degree of intelligence. The decisions affecting matters of general interest come to by an assembly of men of distinction, but specialists in different walks of life, are not sensibly superior to the decisions that would be adopted by a gathering of imbeciles. The truth is, they can only bring to bear in common on the work in hand those mediocre qualities which are the birthright of every average individual. In crowds it is stupidity and not mother-wit that is accumulated. It is not all the world, as is so often repeated, that has more wit than Voltaire, but assuredly Voltaire that has more wit than all the world, if by "all the world" crowds are to be understood.

If the individuals of a crowd confined themselves to putting in common the ordinary qualities of which each of them has his share, there would merely result the striking of an average, and not, as we have said is actually the case, the creation of new characteristics. How is it that these new characteristics are created? This is what we are now to investigate.

Different causes determine the appearance of these characteristics peculiar to crowds, and not possessed by isolated individuals. The first is that the individual forming part of a crowd acquires, solely from numerical considerations, a sentiment of invincible power which allows him to yield to instincts which, had he been alone, he would perforce have kept under restraint. He will be the less disposed to check himself from the consideration that, a crowd being anonymous, and in consequence irresponsible, the sentiment of responsibility which always controls individuals disappears entirely.

The second cause, which is contagion, also intervenes to determine the manifestation in crowds of their special characteristics, and at the same time the trend they are to take. Contagion is a phenomenon of which it is easy to establish the presence, but that it is not easy to explain. It must be classed among those phenomena of a hypnotic order, which we shall shortly study. In a crowd every sentiment and act is contagious, and contagious to such a degree that an individual readily sacrifices his personal interest to the collective interest. This is an aptitude very contrary to his nature, and of which a man is scarcely capable, except when he makes part of a crowd.

A third cause, and by far the most important, determines in the individuals of a crowd special characteristics which are quite contrary at times to those presented by the isolated individual. I allude to that suggestibility of which, moreover, the contagion mentioned above is neither more nor less than an effect.

To understand this phenomenon it is necessary to bear in mind certain recent physiological discoveries. We know today that by various processes an individual may be brought into such a condition that, having entirely lost his conscious personality, he obeys all the suggestions of the operator who has deprived him of it, and commits acts in utter contradiction with his character and habits. The most careful observations seem to prove that an individual immerged for some length of time in a crowd in action soon finds himself—either in consequence of the magnetic influence given out by the crowd, or from some other cause of which we are ignorant—in a special state, which much resembles the state of fascination in which the hypnotised individual finds himself in the hands of the hypnotiser. The activity of the brain being paralysed in the case of the hypnotised subject, the latter becomes the slave of all the unconscious activities of his spinal cord, which the hypnotiser directs at will. The conscious personality has entirely vanished; will and discernment are lost. All feelings and thoughts are bent in the direction determined by the hypnotiser.

Such also is approximately the state of the individual forming part of a psychological crowd. He is no longer conscious of his acts. In his case, as in the case of the hypnotised subject, at the same time that certain faculties are destroyed, others may be brought to a high degree of exaltation. Under the influence of a suggestion, he will undertake the accomplishment of certain acts with irresistible impetuosity. This impetuosity is the more irresistible in the case of crowds than in that of the hypnotised subject, from the fact that, the suggestion being the same for all the individuals of the crowd, it gains in strength by reciprocity. The individualities in the crowd who might possess a personality sufficiently strong to resist the suggestion are too few in number to struggle against the current. At the utmost, they may be able to attempt a diversion by means of different suggestions. It is in this way, for instance, that a happy expression, an image opportunely evoked, have occasionally deterred crowds from the most bloodthirsty acts.

We see, then, that the disappearance of the conscious personality, the predominance of the unconscious personality, the turning by means of suggestion and contagion of feelings and ideas in an identical direction, the tendency to immediately transform the suggested ideas into acts; these, we see, are the principal characteristics of the individual forming part of a crowd. He is no longer himself, but has become an automaton who has ceased to be guided by his will.

Moreover, by the mere fact that he forms part of an organised crowd, a man descends several rungs in the ladder of civilisation. Isolated, he may be a cultivated individual; in a crowd, he is a barbarian—that is, a creature acting by instinct. He possesses the spontaneity, the violence, the ferocity, and also the enthusiasm and heroism of primitive beings, whom he further tends to resemble by the facility with which he allows himself to be impressed by words and images—which would be entirely without action on each of the isolated individuals composing the crowd—and to be induced to commit acts contrary to his most obvious interests and his best-known habits. An individual in a crowd is a grain of sand amid other grains of sand, which the wind stirs up at will.

It is for these reasons that juries are seen to deliver verdicts of which each individual juror would disapprove, that parliamentary assemblies adopt laws and measures of which each of their members would disapprove in his own person. Taken separately, the men of the Convention were enlightened citizens of peaceful habits. United in a crowd, they did not hesitate to give their adhesion to the most savage proposals, to guillotine individuals most clearly innocent, and, contrary to their interests, to renounce their inviolability and to decimate themselves.

It is not only by his acts that the individual in a crowd differs essentially from himself. Even before he has entirely lost his independence, his ideas and feelings have undergone a transformation, and the transformation is so profound as to change the miser into a spendthrift, the sceptic into a believer, the honest man into a criminal, and the coward into a hero. The renunciation of all its privileges which the nobility voted in a moment of enthusiasm during the celebrated night of August 4, 1789, would certainly never have been consented to by any of its members taken singly.

The conclusion to be drawn from what precedes is, that the crowd is always intellectually inferior to the isolated individual, but that, from the point of view of feelings and of the acts these feelings provoke, the crowd may, according to circumstances, he better or worse than the individual. All depends on the nature of the suggestion to which the crowd is exposed. This is the point that has been completely misunderstood by writers who have only studied crowds from the criminal point of view. Doubtless a crowd is often criminal, but also it is often heroic. It is crowds rather than isolated individuals that may be induced to run the risk of death to secure the triumph of a creed or an idea, that may be fired with enthusiasm for glory and honour, that are led on—almost without bread and without arms, as in the age of the Crusades—to deliver the tomb of Christ from the infidel, or, as in '93, to defend the fatherland. Such heroism is without doubt somewhat unconscious, but it is of such heroism that history is made. Were peoples only to be credited with the great actions performed in cold blood, the annals of the world would register but few of them.

Lester Frank Ward

1841-1913

Source: *Applied Sociology* (1906)

Selection: Chapter I: Relation of Pure to Applied Sociology, pp. 3-12

Ward is often described as the "father" of American sociology and the "American Aristotle," although he grew up in a very poor family and was self-taught as a youth. Some believe his impoverished childhood and hard labor in a wagon shop instilled in him an outrage at society's injustice and inequalities. These feelings were reflected in the many pioneering sociological books he wrote that supported the idea of equality of women and of all classes and races in society, which he argued could be achieved through universal education. His writings are largely responsible for the rapid inclusion of sociology courses in colleges and universities throughout America. In 1905, Ward began serving as the editor of the American Journal of Sociology, *and in 1906 and 1907 he served as the first President of the American Sociological Society (which is now known as the American Sociological Association). The writing below, from* Applied Sociology, *published in 1906, shows how Ward distinguished between the roles of sociology as a science and an applied discipline that can be used to achieve positive social change.*

*

The terms "pure" and "applied" should be used in the same sense in social science as in all other sciences. Any apparent differences should be such only as grow out of the nature of social science as the most complex of all sciences, and hence the most difficult to reduce to exact formulas. It is important, therefore, to gain at the outset a clear conception of what is meant by these terms, and especially of the essential distinction between pure and applied sociology. Before proceeding, therefore, to set forth the principles of applied sociology at length, it may be well briefly to define the two branches with the special object of rendering this distinction clear.

Pure Sociology. Pure sociology is simply a scientific inquiry into the actual condition of society. It alone can yield true social self-consciousness. It answers the questions What, Why, and How, by furnishing the facts, the causes, and the principles of sociology. It is a means of self-orientation. When men know what they are, what forces have molded them into their present shape and character, and according to what principles of nature the creative and transforming processes have operated, they begin really to understand themselves. Not only is a mantle of charity thrown over everything that exists, such as virtually to preclude all blame, but a rational basis is now for the first time furnished for considering to what extent and in what manner things that are not in all respects what they would like to have them may be put in the way of such modification as will bring them more into harmony with the desired state. At least it thus, and only thus, becomes possible to distinguish between those social conditions which are susceptible of modification through human action and those that are practically unalterable or are beyond the reach of human agency. In this way an enormous amount of energy otherwise wasted can be saved and concentrated upon the really feasible.

But by far the most important effect of the knowledge furnished by pure sociology is that of showing the difficulty of modifying certain conditions which are not absolutely unalterable, but which, without such knowledge, are supposed capable of easy alteration. In most such cases those who imagine themselves to be sufferers from their presence believe that certain others have them under their control and might alter or abolish them if they were willing to do so. This is the source of the greater part of the bitter class animosity in society. In other words, the most important lesson that pure sociology teaches is that of the great stability of social structures. But it also teaches that few if any social structures are wholly incapable of modification, and the further truth is revealed that in most cases such structures, though they cannot be changed by the direct methods usually applied, may be at least gradually transformed by indirect methods and the adoption of the appropriate means.

Applied sociology, therefore, rests upon pure sociology. If it has any scientific character at all, it presupposes it and proceeds entirely from it. In so far as the idea of reform inheres in applied sociology it can bear no fruit except it so proceeds. Reform may be defined as the desirable modification of social structures. Any attempt to do this must be based on a full knowledge of the nature of such structures, otherwise its failure is certain. Such knowledge includes an acquaintance with the history of the structures to be affected. This history must go back to a time when the structures were not injurious but useful. It must go back to the period of their development in response to external and internal stimuli. Such a period there must have been in every case, otherwise the structures could never have come into existence. In the prosecution of such a research it will not do to be deceived by names. The names of institutions change, sometimes, after ceasing to be longer in harmony with social conditions, acquiring forms descriptive of their real or supposed evil character. Applied sociology looks beneath all this and learns from pure sociology what was their origin, what has been their complete history, and what is their true nature. With such data the question of their modification through the conscious action of society can be intelligently considered, and if, as is usually the case, they cannot be immediately abolished or abruptly changed, the way is made plain for the adoption of indirect means that will secure their gradual transformation and the elimination of their anti-social elements.

All this would mean a complete change in the whole method of reform. With the idea of reform has always thus far been associated that of heat rather than light. Reforms are supposed to emanate from the red end of the social spectrum and to be the product of its thermic and not of its luminous rays. But the method of passion and vituperation produces no effect. It is characteristic of the unscientific method to advocate and of the scientific method to investigate. However ardent the desire for reform may be, it can only be satisfied by dispassionate inquiry, and the realization of the warmest sentiments is only possible through the coldest logic. There either is or has been good in everything. No institution is an unmixed evil. Most of those (such as slavery, for example) that many would gladly see abolished entirely, are defended by some. But both the defenders and the assailants of such institutions usually neglect their history and the causes that created them. The hortatory method deals with theses and antitheses, while the scientific method deals with syntheses. Only by the latter method is it possible to arrive at the truth common to both. Only thus can a rational basis be reached for any effective action looking to the amelioration of social conditions.

Applied Sociology. Just as pure sociology aims to answer the questions What, Why, and How, so applied sociology aims to answer the question What for. The former deals with facts, causes, and principles, the latter with the object, end, or purpose. The one treats the subject-matter of sociology, the other its use. However theoretical pure sociology may be in some of its aspects, applied sociology is essentially practical. It appeals directly to interest. It has to do with social ideals, with ethical considerations, with what ought to be. While pure sociology treats of the "spontaneous development of society," applied sociology "deals with artificial means of accelerating the spontaneous processes of nature." The subject-matter of pure sociology is achievement, that of applied sociology is improvement. The former relates to the past and the present, the latter to the future. Achievement is individual, improvement is social. Applied sociology takes account of artificial phenomena consciously and intentionally directed by society to bettering society. Improvement is social achievement. In pure sociology the point of view is wholly objective. It may be said to relate to social function. In applied sociology the point of view is subjective. It relates to feeling,—the collective well-being. In pure sociology the desires and wants of men are considered as the motor agencies of society. In applied sociology they are considered as sources of enjoyment through their satisfaction. The distinction is similar to that between production and consumption in economics. Indeed, applied sociology may be said to deal with social utility as measured by the satisfaction of desire.

In the analysis of a dynamic action made in Chapter XI of Pure Sociology, the only one of the three effects upon which it was found necessary to dwell was the direct effect of the action in transforming the environment. In applied sociology the only one of these effects considered is the one that was there put first, viz., that of satisfying the desire of the individual. In other words, while in pure sociology the constructive direct effects of human effort only were dealt with, in applied sociology it is the success of such efforts in supplying human wants that is taken into account.

All applied science is necessarily anthropocentric. Sociology is especially so. The old anthropocentric theory which taught that the universe was specially planned in the interest of man is not only false but pernicious in discouraging human effort. But true, scientific anthropocentrism is highly progressive, since it teaches that the universe, although very imperfectly adapted to man's interests, can be so adapted by man himself. Applied sociology is chiefly concerned with enforcing this truth. Throughout the theological and metaphysical stages of human thought philosophy was absorbed in the contemplation of the alleged author of nature. Pure science produced the first change of front, viz., from God to nature. Applied science constitutes a second change of front, viz., from nature to man. Nature is seen to embody utilities and effort is directed to the practical realization of these.

Applied sociology differs from other applied sciences in embracing all men instead of a few. Most of the philosophy which claims to be scientific, if it is not actually pessimistic in denying the power of man to ameliorate his condition, is at least oligocentric in concentrating all effort on a few of the supposed elite of mankind and ignoring or despising the great mass that have not proved their inherent superiority. The question of superiority in general will be considered later, but it may be said here that from the standpoint of applied sociology all men are really equal. Nor is this in the Jeffersonian sense precisely, though it is a sense akin to that, viz., that, whatever may be the differences in their faculties, all men have an equal right to the exercise and enjoyment of the faculties that they have. Applied sociology is egalitarian to the extent of aiming to secure this right for all men equally. It is not only anthropocentric but pancentric.

With a few such exceptions, growing out of the nature of the science (and in this respect it does not differ from other sciences), applied sociology is entirely analogous to other applied sciences. No science can be applied unless it rests on exact mechanical principles. In Pure Sociology (Chapters IX-XI) it was shown that sociology does rest on such principles. Applied sociology assumes that these principles are true, and this work is therefore based on that one and cannot even be understood by one not acquainted with that. It does not, however, follow that the reader must accept as true all the principles laid down in that work. He may question their validity to any extent. But they may be clearly understood without being accepted, and all that is maintained here is that this work cannot be understood unless the principles set forth in that one are also understood.

Science is never exactly the same thing as art. Applied science is therefore not the same as art. If it is art it is not science. A science, whether pure or applied, is a discipline that can be taught more or less fully in a class-room, not necessarily from books, but from books, lectures, and object-lessons. In most sciences, even in the pure stage, field studies are of the highest importance, and in their applied stage it becomes almost essential for the student to apply the principles directly to nature, but this is almost always done in miniature, or on a small scale, for practice only, and without expectation of any practical result. In this way preparation may be made for all the practical arts. But the applied sciences thus taught are not the arts themselves. Applied mathematics is not mensuration, surveying, or engineering. Applied astronomy is not navigation. Applied physics is not manufacture. Applied chemistry is not agriculture. Applied biology leads to a great number of arts, some of which are of very recent origin.

Comte laid down two principles, which, however much they may fall short of universality, are well worthy of attention. One was that the practical applications of the sciences increase with their complexity. This was long rejected with disdain and the superior utility of the physical forces over any of the applications of vital phenomena was pointed to as its conclusive refutation. But are these forces more useful to man than those which have caused the earth to yield its cereals and fruits and have produced domestic animals? And now, with the modern discoveries in bacteriology and kindred branches bringing their incalculable benefits to man, we may well doubt whether even electricity has proved a greater boon.

The other principle was that phenomena grow more susceptible to artificial modification with the increasing complexity of the phenomena. Comte did not illustrate this as fully as he should have done, but his main conclusion from it was that social phenomena are the most susceptible of all to modification. Doubts as to the validity of this principle have been less freely expressed than in case of the one last considered. But it seems to me that they are even more justifiable. Still, it depends here very much upon the point of view. The modification of social phenomena has proved very difficult, while that of physical phenomena seems comparatively easy. But this is a superficial view. The real reason why attempts to modify social phenomena have so often failed is that the phenomena were not understood. It is equally impossible to modify physical phenomena before they are understood. Comte did not say that the complex sciences were more easily understood than the simple ones; on the contrary, he constantly insists on their greater difficulty of comprehension. The principle under consideration, fully stated, would be that, assuming them equally well understood, the modifiability of phenomena is in direct proportion to their complexity. Thus stated, it may be regarded as open to discussion. No adequate attempt has yet been made either to confirm or to disprove it. I am myself disposed to accept it with certain reserves; but this is not the place to discuss it in full.

But the degree to which the application of a science to human uses becomes possible, desirable, or prominent depends rather on the nature of the science than on its position in the hierarchy. Sidereal astronomy has remained for the most part a science of pure contemplation, but there are great possibilities in astrophysics. Nearly all branches of physics have proved useful, but until the discovery of the X-rays spectrum analysis remained a pure science. Chemistry, though applicable to human uses in nearly all its departments, has probably thus far contributed less in this direction than has physics as a whole. Biology has already been mentioned, and its possibilities are immense, but the departments now found to be the most useful are the ones that were unknown a century ago, and long remained fields of mere idle curiosity, regarded as the farthest possible removed from any practical utility. In this respect bacteriology may be compared to electricity. Psychology is now almost exclusively a pure science, but no one dares to say that it will always remain such. That sociology may become an applied science no one will dispute who believes that it is a science at all. And although its phenomena are the most complex of all and the most difficult fully to understand, when understood, if they ever are, the results their study promises in the direction of their modification in the interest of man are beyond calculation.

But applied sociology is not government or politics, nor civic or social reform. It does not itself apply sociological principles; it seeks only to show how they may be applied. It is a science, not an art. The most that it claims to do is to lay down certain general principles as guides to social and political action. But in this it must be exceedingly cautious. The principles can consist only of the highest generalizations. They can have only the most general bearing on current events and the popular or burning questions of the hour. The sociologist who undertakes to discuss these, especially to take sides on them, abandons his science and becomes a politician. A large part of Herbert Spencer's writings is of this character. Much of it is to be found even in his Synthetic Philosophy. It only reflects his prejudices and his feelings, and is not scientific. Moreover, as I have repeatedly shown, it is not in harmony with his system as a whole, but rather in conflict with it.

The same may of course be said of nearly the whole social reform movement embraced under the general term "socialism," and including the utopian schools as well as the practical ones—Fourier as well as Karl Marx. They all seek to bring about modifications in social structures. They would change human institutions more or less radically and abruptly. While the advocates themselves do not attempt, except in a few cases on a small scale, to produce these changes, they seek to create a public sentiment in favor of such changes sufficiently general to secure them through legislation. In so far as they actually succeed in this they accomplish their end. The changes are voted or decreed and the state strives to realize them. But often the institutions fail to yield even to the power of the state, and a long struggle follows, such as France is now having with the parochial schools. But all know in how few cases the social reform party acquires political control. This is on account of the stability of social structures. In old settled countries with definite class interests, prescriptive rights, and large vested interests, this is more clearly seen than in new countries, and hence it is in these latter that social reform movements are most successful. But the statistics show that the socialist vote is increasing in all countries where it is made a political issue, and the time may arrive when the party will come into power somewhat generally.

But all this is politics. It is art and not science. The sociologist has no more quarrel with any of these movements than he has with any other political parties,—Whig, Tory, Democrat, Republican. He observes them all, as he does all social phenomena, but they only constitute data for his science. All that he objects to is that any of these things be called sociology. Misarchism, anarchism, and socialism are programs of political action, negative or positive, and belong to the social art. They are not scientific theories or principles and do not belong to social science.

Superiority of the Artificial. Applied sociology proceeds on the assumption of the superiority of the artificial to the natural. In this, however, it does not differ from any other applied science. What is the meaning of applied science if it be not that it teaches how natural phenomena may be modified by artificial means so as to render them more useful or less injurious to man? The wind that blows over the land, though sometimes destructive, may be useful in many ways, but it will not grind corn. By the adoption of the proper artificial means it may be made to grind corn. As it blows over the sea, though a greater source of danger, it may by artificial devices be made to propel vessels and even to guide them. Water, coming in almost inexhaustible quantities from the mountains or highlands of the interior of large continents, is useful even within the banks of rivers, but by the use of the proper artificial means its usefulness can be multiplied a thousandfold. The same is true of every other element in nature,—wood, clay, stone, metals, light, heat, electricity. The last-named element represents the most extreme case. Although it pervades all space, it produces no appreciable effect except in its violent manifestations as lightning, where the effect is destructive of everything in its way. The whole of its beneficial influence is due to artificial devices. These have been secured through the prolonged study of both the pure and the applied science.

There are some illustrations of the superiority of the artificial outside of the arts proper. One only need be mentioned. Modern languages generally, and the English language in particular, have their individual words more arbitrary than those of the ancient languages. They have less intrinsic meaning and consist more completely of mere symbols. On this account they are more plastic and capable of expressing much finer shades of meaning. But an arbitrary word or a symbol is an artificial product. It is a tool of the mind, devised by the genius of man. It may be said that such words, like everything else in language, are unconsciously developed, and are therefore genetic products. This may be admitted, but it forms no entire exception to other arts, such, for example, as pottery. In fact, the conquest of nature as sketched in the nineteenth chapter of Pure Sociology was mainly a genetic process, but was only possible through the constant exercise of the telic faculty of man. It was the product of individual telesis, and this has always been at work in the formation of language as in all other civilizing processes.

A single example may also be adduced in the domain of collective telesis. Society has also made more or less use of the principle of the superiority of the artificial. In the animal world we see constant illustrations of what is commonly called natural justice, and jurists, statesmen, and philosophers habitually contrast this with what they call civil justice. But natural or animal justice is of course no justice at all, but the absence of justice. There is no natural justice, and all justice is artificial. This constitutes one of the best illustrations of the principle under consideration, and it is especially appropriate here as belonging strictly within the field of applied sociology.

Gabriel Tarde

1843-1904

Source: *The Laws of Imitation* (1903 edition)
Selection: Chapter I: Universal Repetition, pp. 1-13

Tarde was a leading French sociologist, criminologist, and social psychologist who also served during his career as a magistrate, director of the criminal statistics bureau at the Ministry of Justice in Paris, and professor of modern philosophy at the Collège de France. *By 1875 he had developed his basic social theory, which held that invention is the source of all progress, although it is rare among individuals. The innovations are then imitated, which differ in both degree and kind, and subsequently give rise to opposition between adopters of the varied imitations, including those that reflect the new and the old in a culture. This process eventually leads to an adaptation, which is itself an invention. For Tarde, this series of events represented an ongoing cycle that was basic to understanding social history. He explained the process in his 1898 book* Les Lois Socials (Social Laws*), and treated the repetition phase in his best-known work,* Les Lois de l'imitation (The Laws of Imitation, *published in 1890*), *which is presented below. In this writing, Tarde also discusses the nature of the new science of sociology and "social facts," a concept made most famous by Durkheim. Tarde's work influenced later thinking about the concepts of social psychology and the diffusion of social ideas. Among the concepts he initiated were the group mind, which was developed by Le Bon and sometimes used to explain so-called herd behavior or crowd psychology.*

*

Can we have a science or only a history, or, at most, a philosophy of social phenomena? This question is always open. And yet, if social facts are closely observed from a certain point of view, they can be reduced, like other facts, to series of minute and homogeneous phenomena and to the formulas, or laws, which sum up these series. Why, then, is the science of society still unborn, or born but recently, among all its adult and vigorous sister sciences? The chief reason is, I think, that we have thrown away the substance for its shadow and substituted words for things. We have thought it impossible to give a scientific look to *sociology* except by giving it a biological or, better still, a mechanical air. This is an attempt to light up the known by the unknown. It is transforming a solar system into a non-resolvable nebula in order to understand it better.

In social subjects we are exceptionally privileged in having veritable causes, positive and specific acts, at first hand; this condition is wholly lacking in every other subject of investigation. It is unnecessary, therefore, to rely for an explanation of social facts upon those so-called general causes which physicists and naturalists are obliged to create under the name of force, energy, conditions of existence, and other verbal palliatives of their ignorance of the real groundwork of things.

But are we to consider that human acts are the sole factors of history? Surely this is too simple! And so we bind ourselves to contrive other causes on the type of those useful fictions which are elsewhere imposed upon us, and we congratulate ourselves upon being able at times to give an entirely impersonal colour to human phenomena by reason of our lofty, but, truly speaking, obscure, point of view. Let us ward off this vague idealism. Let us likewise ward off the vapid individualism which consists in explaining social changes as the caprices of certain great men. On the other hand, let us explain these changes through the more or less fortuitous appearance, as to time and place, of certain great ideas, or rather, of a considerable number of both major and minor ideas, of ideas which are generally anonymous and usually of obscure birth; which are simple or abstruse; which are seldom illustrious, but which are always novel. Because of this latter attribute, I shall take the liberty of baptising them collectively *inventions* or *discoveries.* By these two terms I mean any kind of an innovation or improvement, however slight, which is made in any previous innovation throughout the range of social phenomena—language, religion, politics, law, industry, or art. At the moment when this novel thing, big or little as it may be, is conceived of, or determined by, an individual, nothing appears to change in the social body,—just as nothing changes in the physical appearance of an organism which a harmful or beneficent microbe has just invaded,—and the gradual changes caused by the introduction of the new element seem to follow, without visible break, upon the anterior social changes into whose current they have glided. Hence arises the illusion which leads philosophers of history into affirming that there is a real and fundamental continuity in historic metamorphoses. The true causes can be reduced to a chain of ideas which are, to be sure, very numerous, but which are in themselves distinct and discontinuous, although they are connected by the much more numerous acts of imitation which are modelled upon them.

Our starting-point lies here in the re-inspiring initiatives which bring new wants, together with new satisfactions, into the world, and which then, through spontaneous and unconscious or artificial and deliberate imitation, propagate or tend to propagate, themselves, at a more or less rapid, but regular, rate, like a wave of light, or like a family of termites. The regularity to which I refer is not in the least apparent in social things until they are resolved into their several elements, when it is found to lie in the simplest of them, in combinations of distinct inventions, in flashes of genius which have been accumulated and changed into commonplace lights. I confess that this is an extremely difficult analysis. Socially, everything is either invention or imitation. And invention bears the same relation to imitation as a mountain to a river. There is certainly nothing less subtle than this point of view; but in holding to it boldly and unreservedly, in exploiting it from the most trivial detail to the most complete synthesis of facts, we may, perhaps, notice how well fitted it is to bring into relief all the picturesqueness and, at the same time, all the simplicity of history, and to reveal historic perspectives which may be characterised by the freakishness of a rock-bound landscape, or by the conventionality of a park walk. This is idealism also, if you choose to call it so; but it is the idealism which consists in explaining history through the ideas of its actors, not through those of the historian.

If we consider the science of society from this point of view, we shall at once see that human sociology is related to animal sociologies, as a species to its genus, so to speak. That it is an extraordinary and infinitely superior species, I admit, but it is allied to the others, nevertheless. M. Espinas expressly states in his admirable work on *Societes animates,* a work which was written long before the first edition of this book, that the labours of ants may be very well explained on the principle "*of individual initiative followed by imitation.*" This initiative is always an innovation or invention that is equal to one of our own in boldness of spirit. To conceive the idea of constructing an arch, or a tunnel, at an appropriate point, an ant must be endowed with an innovating instinct equal to, or surpassing, that of our canal-digging or mountain-tunnelling engineers. [. . .] In view of the fact that modification of instinct is probably related to the same principle as the genesis and modification of species, we may be tempted to enquire whether the principle of the imitation of invention, or of something physiologically analogous, would not be the clearest possible explanation of the ever-open problem of the origin of species. But let us leave this question and confine ourselves to the statement that both animal and human societies may be explained from this point of view.

In the second place, and this is the special thesis of this chapter, the subject of social science is seen, from this standpoint, to present a remarkable analogy to the other domains of general science, and, in this way, to become re-embodied, so to speak, in the rest of the universe, where it had before this the air of an outsider.

In every field of study, affirmations pure and simple enormously outnumber explanations. And, in all cases, the first data are simply affirmed; they are the extraordinary and accidental facts, the premises and sources from which proceeds all that which is subsequently explained. The astronomer states that certain nebulae, certain celestial bodies of a given mass and volume and at a given distance, exist, or have existed. The chemist makes the same statement about certain chemical substances, the physicist, about certain kinds of ethereal vibrations, which he calls light, electricity, and magnetism; the naturalist states that there are certain principal organic types, to begin with, plants and animals; the physiographer states that there are certain mountain chains, which he calls the Alps, the Andes, *et cetera.* In teaching us about these capital facts from which the rest are deduced, are these investigators doing the work, strictly speaking, of scientists? They are not; they are merely affirming certain facts, and they in no way differ from the historian who chronicles the expedition of Alexander or the discovery of printing. If there be any difference, it is, as we shall see, wholly to the advantage of the historian. What, then, do we know in the scientific sense of the word? Of course, we answer that we know causes and effects. And when we have learned that, in the case of two different events, the one is the outcome of the other, or that both collaborate towards the same end, we say that they have been explained. But let us imagine a world where there is neither resemblance nor repetition, a strange, but, if need be, an intelligible hypothesis; a world where everything is novel and unforeseen, where the creative imagination, unchecked by memory, has full play, where the motions of the stars are sporadic, where the agitations of the ether are unrhythmical, and where successive generations are without the common traits of an hereditary type. And yet every apparition in such a phantasmagoria might be produced and determined by another, and might even, in its turn, become the cause of others. In such a world causes and effects might still exist; but would any kind of a science be possible? It would not be, because, to reiterate, neither resemblances nor repetitions would be found there.

This is the essential point. Knowledge of causes is sometimes sufficient for foresight; but knowledge of resemblances always allows of enumeration and measurement, and science depends primarily upon number and measure.

More than this is, of course, necessary. As soon as a new science has staked out its field of characteristic resemblances and repetitions, it must compare them and note the bond of solidarity which unites their concomitant variations. But, as a matter of fact, the mind does not fully understand nor clearly recognise the relation of cause and effect, except in as much as the effect resembles or repeats the cause, as, for example, when a sound wave produces another sound wave, or a cell, another cell. There is nothing more mysterious, one may say, than such reproductions. I admit this; but when we have once accepted this mystery, there is nothing clearer than the resulting series. [. . .]

When like things form parts of the same or of supposedly the same whole, like the molecules of a volume of hydrogen, or the woody cells of a tree, or the soldiers of a regiment, the resemblance is referred to as a quantity instead of a group. In other words, when the things *which repeat themselves* remain united as they increase, like vibrations of heat or electricity, accumulating within some heated or electrified object, or like cells multiplying in the body of a growing child, or like proselytes to a common religion, in such cases the repetition is called a growth instead of a series. In all of this I fail to see anything which would differentiate the subject of social science.

Besides, whether resemblances and repetitions are intrinsic or extrinsic, quantities or groups, growths or series, they are the necessary themes of the differences and variations which exist in all phenomena. They are the canvas of their embroidery, the measure of their music. The wonder world which I was picturing would be, at bottom, the least richly differentiated of all possible worlds. How much greater a renovator than revolution is our modern industrial system, accumulation as it is of mutually imitative actions! What is more monotonous than the free life of the savage in comparison with the hemmed-in life of civilised man? Would any organic progress be possible without heredity? Would the exuberant variety of geological ages and of living nature have sprung into existence independently of the periodicity of the heavenly motions or of the wave-like rhythm of the earth's forces?

Repetition exists, then, for the sake of variation. Otherwise, the necessity of death (a problem which M. Delbceuf considers in his book upon animate and inanimate matter, almost impossible of solution), would be incomprehensible; for why should not the top of life spin on, after it was wound up, forever? But under the hypothesis that repetitions exist only to embody all the phases of a certain unique originality which seeks expression, death must inevitably supervene after all these variations have been fully effected. I may note in this connection, in passing, that the relation of universal to particular, a relation which fed the entire philosophic controversy of the Middle Ages upon nominalism and realism, is precisely that of repetition to variation. *Nominalism* is the doctrine in accordance with which individual characteristics or idiosyncracies are the only significant realities. *Realism,* on the other hand, considers only those traits worthy of attention and of the name of reality through which a given individual resembles other individuals and tends to reproduce himself in them. The interest of this kind of speculation is apparent when we consider that in politics individualism is a special kind of nominalism, and socialism, a special kind of realism.

All repetition, social, vital, or physical, *i. e., imitative, hereditary,* or *vibratory* repetition (to consider only the most salient and typical forms of universal repetition), springs from some innovation, just as every light radiates from some central point, and thus throughout science the normal appears to originate from the accidental. For the propagation of an attractive force or luminous vibration from a heavenly body, or of a race of animals from an ancestral pair, or of a national idea or desire or religious rite from a scholar or inventor or missionary, seem to us like natural and regular phenomena; whereas we are constantly surprised by the strange and partly non-formulable sequence or juxtaposition of their respective centres, *i.e.,* the different crafts, religions, and social institutions, the different organic types, the different chemical substances or celestial masses from which all these radiations have issued. All these admirable uniformities or series,—hydrogen, whose multitudinous, star-scattered atoms are universally homogeneous, protoplasm, identical from one end to the other of the scale of life, the roots of the Indo-European languages, identical almost throughout civilisation, the expansion of the light of a star in the immensity of space, the unbroken sequence from geological times of incalculable generations of marine species, the wonderfully faithful transmission of words from the Coptic of the ancient Egyptians to us moderns, etc.,—all these innumerable masses of things of like nature and of like affiliations, whose harmonious co-existence or equally harmonious succession we admire, are related to physical, biological, and social accidents by a tie which baffles us.

Here, also, the analogy between social and natural phenomena is carried out. But we should not be surprised if the former seem chaotic when we view them through the medium of the historian, or even through that of the sociologist, whereas the latter impress us, as they are presented by physicist, chemist, or physiologist, as very well ordered worlds. These latter scientists show us the subject of their science only on the side of its characteristic resemblances and repetitions; they prudently conceal its corresponding heterogeneities and transformations (or trans-substantiations). The historian and sociologist, on the contrary, veil the regular and monotonous face of social facts,—that part in which they are alike and repeat themselves,—and show us only their accidental and interesting, their infinitely novel and diversified, aspect. If our subject were, for example, the Gallo-Romans, the historian, even the philosophic historian, would not think of leading us step by step through conquered Gaul in order to show us how every word, rite, edict, profession, custom, craft, law, or military manoeuvre, how, in short, every special idea or need which had been introduced from Rome had begun to spread from the Pyrenees to the Rhine, and to win its way, after more or less vigorous fighting against old Celtic customs and ideas, to the mouths and arms and hearts and minds of all the enthusiastic Gallic imitators of Rome and Caesar. At any rate, if our historian had once led us upon this long journey, he would not make us repeat it for every Latin word or grammatical form, for every ritualistic form in the Roman religion, for every military manoeuvre that was taught to the legionaries by their officer-instructors, for every variety of Roman architecture, for temple, basilica, theatre, hippodrome, aqueduct, and atriumed villa, for every school-taught verse of Virgil or Horace, for every Roman law, or for every artistic or industrial process in Roman civilisation that had been faithfully and continuously transmitted from pedagogues and craftsmen to pupils and apprentices. And yet it is only at this price that we can get at an exact estimate of the great amount of regularity which obtains in even the most fluctuating societies.

Then, after the introduction of Christianity, our historian would certainly refrain from making us renew this tedious peregrination in connection with every Christian rite which propagated itself, in spite of resistance, through heathen Gaul, like a wave of sound through air that is already in vibration. Instead of this, he would inform us at what date Julius Caesar conquered Gaul, or, again, at what date certain saints came to that country to preach Christianity. He might also enumerate the diverse elements out of which the Roman civilisation and the Christian faith and morality that were introduced into the Gallic world, were composed. In this case, his problem is to understand and rationally, logically, and scientifically, describe the extraordinary superposition of Christianity upon Romanism, or rather, the gradual process of Christian upon the gradual process of Roman assimilation. In the separate treatment of both Romanism and Christianity, he will meet with an equally difficult problem in giving a rational explanation of the strange juxtaposition of the very heterogeneous Etruscan, Greek, Oriental, and other fragments which constituted the former, and of the incoherent Jewish, Egyptian, and Byzantine ideas, ideas which were incoherent even in each distinct group, which constituted the latter. This, however, is the arduous task which the philosopher of history sets before himself and which he thinks that he cannot slur over if he is to do the work of a scholar. He will, therefore, wear himself out in trying to bring order out of disorder by discovering some law or reason for these historic chances and coincidences. He would do better to investigate how and why harmonies sometimes proceed from these coincidences and in what these harmonies consist. I will undertake to do this further on.

In short, a historian of this kind is like the botanist who would feel bound to ignore everything about the generation of plants of the same species or variety, as well as everything about their growth or nutrition, a kind of cellular generation or regeneration of tissues; or like the physicist who disdained to study the propagation of light or heat or sound waves as they passed through different mediums which were themselves in vibration. Can we conceive of the former believing that the proper and exclusive object of his science was an interlinking of unlike species, beginning with the first alga and ending with the last orchid, plus a profound justification of such a concatenation? Can we conceive of the latter convinced that the sole end of his studies was investigation into the reason why there were precisely seven known kinds of luminous undulation, and why, including electricity and magnetism, there were no other kinds of ethereal vibration? These are certainly interesting questions, but although they are open to philosophic, they are not open to scientific, discussion, since their solution does not seem capable of admitting of that high kind of probability which science exacts. It is clear that the first condition of becoming an anatomist or physiologist is the study of tissues, the aggregates of homogeneous cells and fibres and blood vessels, or the study of functions, the accumulations of minute homogeneous contractions, innervations, oxidations, or deoxidations, and then, and above all, belief in the great architect of life, in heredity. It is equally clear that it is of primary importance to the chemist and physicist to examine many kinds of gaseous, liquid, and solid masses, masses composed of corpuscles which are absolutely alike, or of so-called physical forces which are prodigious accumulations of minute, homogeneous vibrations. In fact, in the physical world, everything refers, or is in course of being referred, to vibration. Here everything is taking on more and more an essentially vibratory character, just as in the animate world the reproductive faculty, or the property of transmitting the smallest peculiarities (which are usually of unknown origin) through inheritance, is coming more and more to be thought inherent in the smallest cell.

And now my readers will realise, perhaps, that the social being, in the degree that he is social, is essentially imitative, and that imitation plays a role in societies analogous to that of heredity in organic life or to that of vibration among inorganic bodies. If this is so, it ought to be admitted, in consequence, that a human invention, by which a new kind of imitation is started or a new series opened,—the invention of gunpowder, for example, or windmills, or the Morse telegraph,—stands in the same relation to social science as the birth of a new vegetal or mineral species (or, on the hypothesis of a gradual evolution, of each of the slow modifications to which the new species is due), to biology, or as the appearance of a new mode of motion comparable with light or electricity, or the formation of a new substance, to physics or chemistry. Therefore, if we are to make a just comparison, we must not compare the philosophic historian who strives to discover a law for the odd groups and sequences of scientific, industrial, aesthetic, and political inventions, to the physiologist or physicist, as we know him, to Tyndall or Claude Bernard, but to a philosopher of nature like Schelling or like Haeckel in his hours of riotous imagination.

We should then perceive that the crude incoherence of historic facts, all of which facts are traceable to the different currents of imitation of which they are the point of intersection, a point which is itself destined to be more or less exactly copied, is no proof at all against the fundamental regularity of social life or the possibility of a social science. Indeed, parts of this science exist in the petty experience of each of us, and we have only to piece the fragments together. Besides, a group of historic events would certainly be far from appearing more incoherent than a collection of living types or chemical substances. Why then should we exact from the philosopher of history the fine symmetrical and rational order that we do not dream of demanding from the philosopher of science? And yet there is a distinction here which is entirely to the credit of the historian. It is but recently that the naturalist has had any glimpses that were at all clear of biological evolution, whereas the historian was long ago aware of the continuity of history. As for chemists and physicists, we may pass them by. They dare not even yet forecast the time when they will be able to trace out, in their turn, the genealogy of simple substances, or when a work on the origin of atoms, as successful as Darwin's *Origin of Species,* will be published. It is true that M. Lecoq de Boisbaudran and M. Mendelejeff thought that they had distinguished a natural series of simple substances, and it is true that Boisbaudran's discovery of *gallium* was made in connection with his eminently philosophic speculations along this line. But close consideration, perhaps neither the remarkable attempts of these scientists nor the various systems of our evolutionists on the genealogical ramification of living types present any greater degree of precision or certainty than sparkles in the ideas of Herbert Spencer, or even in those of Vico, upon the so-called periodic and predestined evolutions of society. The origin of atoms is much more mysterious than the origin of species, and the origin of species is, in turn, more mysterious than the origin of civilisations. We can compare extant living species with those which have preceded them, the remains of which we find in the earth's strata; but we have not the slightest trace of the chemical substances which must have preceded, in prehistoric astronomy, so to speak, in the unfathomable and unimaginable depths of the past, the actual chemical substances of the earth and stars. Consequently, chemistry, which cannot even propound a problem of origins, is less advanced, in this essential particular, than biology; and, for like reason, biology is, in reality, less advanced than sociology.

From the foregoing, it is evident that social science and social philosophy are distinct; that social science must deal exclusively, like every other science, with a multitude of homogeneous facts, with those facts which are carefully concealed by the historians; that new and heterogeneous facts, or historical facts, strictly speaking, are the special domain of social philosophy; that from this point of view social science might be as advanced as the other sciences, and that social philosophy is actually much more so than any other philosophy.

Franklin Henry Giddings

1855-1931

Source: *Inductive Sociology* (1901)
Selection: Chapter III: The Consciousness of Kind, pp. 91-101

Giddings was an American sociologist and economist who began his career writing newspaper items. In 1892 he became vice president of the American Academy of Political and Social Science, and in 1894 was offered a new department chair in sociology and the history of civilization at Columbia University, which he developed with great success until he retired in 1928. Toward the end of his career, Giddings was a pioneer in encouraging the use of careful quantitative and experimental methods in studying social phenomena. He conceived of sociology as the study of developing forms of human society, based on the changing intensity of "consciousness of kind," his most well-known concept. It refers to a state of mind whereby one person recognizes another as being of like mind, characterized by collective feelings of similarity and belonging. As a result of association and conflict, consciousness of kind develops through communication, imitation, toleration, co-operation, and alliance. Eventually the group achieves a self-consciousness of its own (as opposed to individual self-consciousness) from which traditions and social values can arise. These concepts are explicated in the following writing from Giddings's 1901 book Inductive Sociology.

*

Organic Sympathy. Before there is any distinct perception of differences or of resemblances by individuals who, from time to time, are brought into contact with one another, there are in their minds differences or resemblances of sensation corresponding to differences or resemblances of response to stimulus. In each mind also are differences or resemblances between sensations awakened by self and sensations awakened by fellow beings, (furthermore, in each mind there are vague feelings of repulsion or of attraction, and equally vague feelings of agreeableness or of disagreeableness in the presence of other persons). Collectively, the resembling sensations of resembling individuals, the resembling sensations of self and of others who resemble self, and the accompanying vague feelings of attraction and of pleasure may be designated by the phrase Organic Sympathy.

Like Feelings with Like Response.—The basis of organic sympathy is the mental and practical resemblance itself.

The original element in organic sympathy is the resemblance of the complex of sensations in one mind to the complex of sensations in another mind, accompanying the like response of the two similar nervous organizations to the same or like stimuli.

Similarity of Sensations of Self and Others.—On this basis, experience creates groupings of other resembling sensations which are antecedent to perceptions of likeness, but which prepare the way for them.

Passing his hands over his mother's face, the infant experiences sensations of pressure that are similar to the sensations that he receives when passing his hands over his own face; but when he strokes the back of the cat, or clutches the hair of the dog, he receives sensations unlike those that he experienced when feeling his own face. From his own voice and the voices of his brothers and sisters, he receives auditory sensations that are alike; but different from these are the sensations aroused by the barking of the dog, or the mewing of the cat. In like manner, the sensations of vision and of smell that are awakened by his own bodily organism, and by the bodily organisms of persons resembling himself, are alike; while between these sensations and those awakened by various animals, the difference is conspicuous. So, throughout life, the child growing into the man is continually receiving from his own bodily organism, and from the closely resembling bodily organisms of individuals like himself, sensations that are in a high degree alike; while sensations different from these are being received from other objects of every kind.

Facility of Imitation.—Animals or persons that closely resemble one another in nervous organization imitate one another with facility.

Often imitation is incited by conspicuous difference, but the greater the difference between one organism and another, the more difficult is any imitation of one by the other. Like response to like stimulus easily develops into an imitation, in minor matters—in details of difference—of one another by creatures that, on the whole, are alike rather than unlike.

Sensations of Meeting.—When two persons who have never before seen one another unexpectedly meet, something happens in the nervous organization of each which, when examined, would have to be described as a physical shock, and something happens in the consciousness of each which would have to be described as either a shock of unpleasant feeling, or as a thrill of pleasurable feeling.

The feeling of shock, surprise, anger, disgust, which may happen to be the experience in the case, is due to a very complicated impression of unlikeness which the stranger makes. The impression is composed of sensations of many kinds: sensations of sight, sensations of hearing, perhaps, also, sensations of odour and of touch. The man's appearance, as seen with the eye, may be repellent or threatening; his voice may grate unpleasantly on the ear; the touch of his hand may create something closely akin to a shudder.

When, however, the experience is a thrill of pleasure, the effect is produced by a complex combination of impressions of unlikeness with impressions of likeness; namely, impressions of the difference of the stranger from the person who encounters him, with impressions of his apparent resemblance. It is instantly clear that this hitherto unknown individual has his own distinctive personality; he is in many respects, perhaps in outward appearance, perhaps in tone of voice, almost certainly in mind and character, different from the one who confronts him. At the same time, there is something recognizable and familiar about him. The fundamental resemblances of the two persons are sufficiently great to dominate their differences, which, for the moment, become relatively unimportant.

It is quite possible for the first impression made by a stranger to awaken little more than sensation and emotion. Thoughts, ideas, perceptions, in the strict meaning of these words, may hardly enter into the matter at all. The mere sensations of meeting, then, may be analyzed, observed, and recorded, as disagreeable or agreeable.

TABLE XXVI.— SENSATIONS OF MEETING

M 1. Disagreeable.	M 2. Agreeable.

Information must be obtained from records made by individual observers.

Total Organic Sympathy.—All of the phenomena above described enter into the composition of that vague but positive state, organic sympathy.

Similarities of sensation in general in the minds of resembling individuals; similarities of sensation of self and of others resembling self; spontaneous imitations, easily effected among like individuals because their differences are trifling in comparison with their resemblances; and sensations of meeting that on the whole are agreeable; these collectively develop into that attraction for one another which is daily seen among resembling men, as it is also among resembling animals, and which lies deeper in consciousness than any clear perception of resemblance. Creatures that presumably have no power of intellectual discrimination manifest the attractions of organic sympathy. Human beings quite capable of nice discrimination often find themselves liking or disliking one another when they can give no reason for their feeling.

Degrees of Organic Sympathy.—The careful observer will not fail to discover that human beings differ among themselves in their power of organic sympathy. In some persons organic sympathy is strong, in others of medium strength, in others weak.

These terms, like many that have already been used in these pages, are purely relative. To give them meaning for purposes of measurement, the observer must take as his standard of strong organic sympathy some one individual or type whose characteristics admit of careful observation and description. One possible standard for organic sympathy is the organic sympathy of mother and babe.

TABLE XXVII.—DEGREES OF ORGANIC SYMPATHY

M 1. Strong.	M 2. Medium.	M 3. Weak.

Information must be obtained from records made by individual observers.

Perception of Resemblance. When the child begins to combine sensations of the moment with memories of similar sensations in the past, and to connect these immediate and memory sensations with the objects that have produced them, the process of perception has begun. The child now has not only like and unlike sensations, but also Perceptions of Likeness and Unlikeness. These are much more complicated mental states.

Perceptions of Difference and of Resemblance.—It seems probable that perceptions of unlikeness appear earlier in the experience of every individual than perceptions of likeness. Indeed, likeness can be distinguished from absolute identity only by perceptions of the differences that exist between things that are in certain respects alike.

In the process of becoming acquainted, the differences between one individual and another are first observed; and a sense of difference is always present in the mind to be more or less overcome by any growing sense of similarity.

As individuals differ in their power of organic sympathy, so do they differ also in their power to perceive differences and resemblances. Some men's perceptions are keen, some are of medium acuteness, some are dull. Before recording and tabulating observations a standard of comparison must be chosen and described.

TABLE XXVIII.—DEGREES OF PERCEPTION OF DIFFERENCE AND RESEMBLANCE

M 1. Keen.	M 2. Medium.	M 3. Dull.

Information must be obtained from records made by individual observers.

Impressions of Meeting.—With the attainment of clear perceptions of differences and resemblances, the mere sensations of meeting are merged in complex Impressions of Meeting. On the intellectual side these are impressions of difference or impressions of resemblance. Accompanying these, however, are emotional states, which are manifested in the attitude of strangers toward one another.

Attitude toward Strangers.—According as the impressions are, on the whole, impressions of difference or impressions of resemblance, the general attitude of strangers toward one another is one of wonder and curiosity; of fear, suspicion, and unfriendliness; of indifference; or of trust and friendliness. Observations should be made of all these emotional manifestations.

TABLE XXIX.—ATTITUDE TOWARD STRANGERS

M 1. Wonder.	M 5. Suspicion.
M 2. Curiosity.	M 6. Trust.
M 3. Indifference.	M 7. Friendliness.
M 4. Fear.	M 8. Unfriendliness.

Information must be obtained from records made by individual observers.

The Motives of Communication.—The first impressions of meeting are usually confused. Impressions of difference and impressions of resemblance are so mingled in the mind that one is left in doubt as to the real degree of resemblance and the possible interest and pleasure of further acquaintance. The desire to impart and to gain a more definite knowledge on these points is the original motive of communication.

The desire to impart must probably be placed first. In all communication we can discover in each communicating person a desire to make an impression. Subordinate to this desire, in most instances, appears to be the desire to know well the other person.

After acquaintance is established much communication takes place, which seems to spring from an interest in the subject that is talked about. We give and ask information about third parties or material things, as well as about ourselves. Even then, however, the other motives that have been mentioned can always be detected; and it is probable that in all cases they are really the predominant ones, although we are not always conscious of the fact.

TABLE XXX.—THE MOTIVES OF COMMUNICATION

M 1. To Perfect Acquaintance by Impression.

M 2. To Perfect Acquaintance by Learning about Another.

M 3. To Gain or Impart Information.

Information must be obtained from records made by individual observers.

Reflective Sympathy. When the perception of resemblance has arisen in consciousness, it reacts upon organic sympathy, and converts or develops it into an Intelligent or Reflective Sympathy.

Reflective sympathy is awakened by the distinct knowledge that another person is like one's self.

The phenomenon was first clearly and accurately described by Spinoza, in the "Ethic," Part III, Prop. XXVII.

> "Although we may not have been moved toward a thing by any affect, yet, if it is like ourselves, whenever we imagine it to be affected by any affect, we are therefore affected by the same. [. . .] If, therefore, the nature of the external body be like that of our body, then the idea of the external body which we imagine will involve an affection of our body like that of the external body. Therefore, if we imagine any one who is like ourselves to be affected with any affect, this imagination will express an affection of our body like that affect; and, therefore, we shall be affected with a similar affect ourselves, because we imagine something like us to be affected with the same."

In other words, when we perceive that some one who is organized as we are is doing a certain thing, we feel the impulse to act as he acts. If he appears to be in pain, we feel a certain discomfort or even a certain degree of the pain that he experiences. If he is evidently in a state of great joy, we also feel a certain degree of gladness.

The relative degrees of reflective sympathy should be observed and estimated according to the method explained for the estimation of degrees of organic sympathy, and perceptions of difference and resemblance.

TABLE XXXI.—DEGREES OF REFLECTIVE SYMPATHY

M 1. Strong. M 2. Medium. M 3. Weak.

Information must be obtained from records made by individual observers.

Affection. The perception of resemblance and conscious sympathy commonly develop into the "stronger feeling" which is variously named Liking, Friendliness, and Affection, according to the degree of its strength. Those individuals who, as we say, have something in common, that is, those who are so much alike that they are sympathetic and have similar ideas and tastes, on the whole like one another better than individuals who have little or nothing in common.

We must not make the mistake, however, of supposing that in all cases the strongest affection springs up between persons who, at the moment of their first acquaintance, are actually very much alike in mental and moral qualities. Perhaps the more frequent case is that of a growing affection between persons potentially alike. Apparently it is the capacity of two or more persons to become alike in mental and moral nature, under each other's influence, that gives rise to the strongest friendship and the highest degree of pleasure in companionship.

Degrees of affection as strong, medium, or weak should be observed and estimated by the method heretofore described for the estimation of the degrees of organic sympathy.

TABLE XXXII.—DEGREES OF AFFECTION

M 1. Strong. M 2. Medium. M 3. Weak.

Information must be obtained from records made by individual observers.

Desire for Recognition. A remaining mental fact to be noted as a subjective consequence of resemblance, is the desire which an individual feels for Recognition, including a return of sympathy and affection.

This phenomenon also was first clearly described by Spinoza in Prop. XXXIII of Part III of the "Ethic": "If we love a thing which is like ourselves, we endeavour as much as possible to make it love us in return."

When a person perceives that his acquaintance resembles himself in mind and character, and is conscious of a certain sympathy and affection for his acquaintance, he looks for some manifestation of interest in himself. He expects the acquaintance also to recognize the points of similarity, and to show feelings of sympathy and liking. This state of mind is the basis of some of the most important passions, such as pride and ambition.

The relative degrees of the desire for recognition should be observed and estimated by the method explained for the estimation of the degrees of organic sympathy.

TABLE XXXIII.—DEGREES OF DESIRE FOR RECOGNITION

M 1. Strong.	M 2. Medium.	M 3. Weak.

Information must be obtained from records made by individual observers.

The Total Consciousness of Kind. The five modes of consciousness which have been described are not independent of one another. They are so intimately blended that it is only by a process of scientific analysis that they can be thought of singly. In actual experience they are united in a state of mind that for the moment seems perfectly simple. The perception of resemblance, the sympathy, the affection, and the desire for recognition that go with it, seem, for the time being, to be as perfectly one fact of consciousness as does the image of a person or of a landscape upon the retina of the eye. This state of consciousness is pleasurable, and includes the feeling that we wish to maintain it and expand it. The feeling that it carries with it is, in fact, like that which one experiences while engaged in a pleasurable game or witnessing an engrossing drama. One does not stop to ask whether it is useful or worth while any more than he does when eagerly looking forward to the next successful move on a chessboard. He enjoys it while it lasts, and feels that it is worth while in itself, quite irrespective of any consequences that may follow.

The consciousness of kind, then, is that pleasurable state of mind which includes organic sympathy, the perception of resemblance, conscious or reflective sympathy, affection, and the desire for recognition.

There are two groups of indications of the consciousness of kind in any community which may be made use of for the purpose of estimating extent and degree. One group is made up of the words and phrases in common use significant of a consciousness of kind. The other group is made up of common acts and prejudices of like significance.

The observer should not begin his search for these indications with a list already made in his own mind. Rather, as he encounters expressions and observes acts which at the moment strike him as having significance as such indications, he should record and classify them, and then make up his lists from materials so obtained.

TABLE XXXIV.—WORDS AND PHRASES IN COMMON USE SIGNIFICANT OF A CONSCIOUSNESS OF KIND

M 1. Very few	M 3. Numerous
M 2. Few	M 4. Very Numerous

TABLE XXXV.—COMMON ACTS AND PREJUDICES SIGNIFICANT OF A CONSCIOUSNESS OF KIND

M 1. Very Few	M 3. Numerous
M 2. Few	M 4. Very Numerous

Information must be obtained from records made by individual observers.

Consciousness of Potential Resemblance. A relatively perfect consciousness of kind can exist only in minds that are in a high degree alike. In every population, however, a large proportion of its component individuals, not yet in a high degree mentally alike, are gradually becoming alike. The consciousness of Potential Resemblance which may be observed in minds that are thus developing into resemblance is a phenomenon of the social mind not less important than the consciousness of kind already relatively perfect.

Potential Resemblance.—We all know from personal experience that there are some minds among our acquaintances that never become more sympathetic with our own. The oftener we engage in argument with them the further apart do they and we seem to drift. With other minds the case is wholly different. The ripening of acquaintance is the ripening of sympathy and agreement. Our differences disappear or become of little consequence. We learn to see things in the same light and to regard them with the same feelings. This organization of two or more minds which makes their approach or agreement certain, is the thing which is meant by the term "potential resemblance."

The Consciousness of Mental Approach.—Accordingly, the consciousness of potential resemblance is a subjective phenomenon somewhat more complex than the consciousness of kind as thus far described. It includes the ordinary perceptions of difference and of resemblance; but combined with these is the further perception that the differences are decreasing and the resemblances increasing; or, perhaps, the judgment that the differences probably will decrease and the resemblances increase. As potential resemblance develops into actual and perfected resemblance, the consciousness of potential resemblance becomes a relatively perfect consciousness of kind.

Ferdinand Tönnies

1855-1936

Source: *Gemeinschaft und Gesellschaft* (1920 edition)
Selection: Results and Prospects, pp. 199-205

The German sociologist Ferdinand Tönnies was a prolific writer and co-founder of the German Society for Sociology. His lifetime work comprises at least 900 published writings covering all major aspects of sociology, including pure theory and the descriptive and methodological aspects of sociological research. Although he was less influential than his German contemporaries Weber and Simmel, Tönnies remains a respected founding father of sociology. In his first book, Gemeinschaft und Gesellschaft *(originally published in 1887), Tönnies presented his most famous contribution to social thought. The title of that work has been variously translated into English as "Community and Society,""Community and Association," and "Community and Civil Society," but some other interpreters claim none of these English terms can quite capture the meaning of the German terms, and for this reason we have left the German terms in our translation. This book is perhaps the first systematic sociological account to sketch an evolution from ancient to modern society. It also includes a social psychological perspective, by conceiving of social formations as expressions of the human will, specifically either of "essential-will" (*Wesenwille*), which is dominant in* Gemeinschaft, *or "arbitrary-will" (*Kürwille*), which is dominant in* Gesellschaft. *These and other seminal concepts are presented in the writing below from the "Results and Prospects" section, which summarizes in a few pages the complex thesis of* Gemeinschaft und Gesellschaft.

*

1. A contrast exists between a social order founded on a consensus, or harmony of wills, which matures and is dignified by tradition, morality, and religion, and a social order founded on the joining together of rational wills, which functions through convention and agreement, and is defended by political laws justified ideologically through public opinion.

With regard to legal systems, in the former type of social order there is a system of common, binding, positive law, of obligatory norms that regulate the interaction of wills. Its roots rest in both the life of the family and the ownership of land. Customs and moral codes primarily determine its forms. The forms, furthermore, are sanctified and exalted by religion as if created by a divine will, or at the least such a will as interpreted by wise rulers. This normative system contrasts sharply with another, similar system of positive law, which maintains the distinct identity of all the individual rational wills as they engage in their complex interactions, including those that are confusing or embarrassing. While the usual order of trade and associated activities give rise to the latter system of positive law, it is the power of the sovereign state that validates the system and gives it its final authority. This kind of law, therefore, not only becomes a very significant policy instrument, but it also maintains, obstructs, or advances social trends. Through public debate such law is defended or attacked, often by dogma and opinion, and in this way it can be changed in the direction of severity or compassion.

In addition, there are also two conceptions of morality, as a wholly ideal or rational system of codified ways to live together. As regards the former, morality primarily expresses religious beliefs and impulses, and is thus necessarily bound up with the circumstances and realities of family life, traditions and customs. As regards the latter, morality totally derives from and is in the service of public opinion, which includes social relationship that are based on contracts, sociability, and political motivations.

We can say law that results from the natural order of things is natural law, law that results from daily affairs = positive law, and law that derives from mores = ideal law. Law is the object of social will when it reflects the sense of what can or should be, of what is intended or tolerable. Even the natural law must be acknowledged as positive and compulsory to be considered valid and real. It is positive, however, in a more universal or less specific way. Compared to special laws it is universal, and compared to complex, intricate laws it is simple.

2. Social life and the social will essentially consist of agreement, customs, morality, and religion, and their various forms develop under favorable societal conditions during the life of society. Each person therefore derives his rewards from the shared life of society, which express themselves uniquely through each individual's emotions, mind, heart, and conscience, as well as in his surroundings, material goods, and behaviors. The same holds for every group. Each person's power is rooted in this societal core, and so are his rights, which derive, in the last analysis, from the sole natural law, which in its heavenly and pure character protect and nourish him, in the same way that it gave him life and

will ordain his death. In certain circumstances and relationships, however, an individual may seem to be free, to self-determine his activities, and thus he should be considered an independent person. In this case, the essence of the communal spirit has become enfeebled or the bond that joins one individual with another has become so weak that they no longer act as a force. In contrast to the family and other types of co-operative relationships, this dissolution applies to all relationships between disconnected individuals who lack both a common understanding and traditional customs or beliefs that can create common bonds. The result is war and the unrestrained freedom of every person to kill and enslave any other person, or, if it better serve their interests, to conclude agreements and form new alliances. While such relationships may exist between restricted groups or communities, and involve their individual members, either in relationship with each other or with others, those types of situations fall outside the scope of this investigation. Rather, here we are concerned with communal organizations and social conditions wherein the members stay isolated from and disguise their animosity toward each, and where only fear of clever revenge prevents them from attacking one another; therefore, even relationships that appear peaceful and friendly exist, in reality, within a potentially warlike situation. According to our definitions, this is the state of *Gesellschaft*-like civilization, in which underlying mutual fear expressed through convention sustains peace and trade. This type of society is safeguarded by the state through laws and politics. Both science and public opinion, to a certain extent, try to define this situation as both necessary and timeless, and to ennoble it as a sign of progress towards some state of perfection.

It is, however, the organization and culture of the *Gemeinschaft* that best allows the traditional character and way of life of a people to persist. The state reflects and represents *Gesellschaft*, and thus opposes those who secretly have hatred and contempt of it, especially if the state has become distanced and alienated from traditional forms of communal culture. Similarly, we find in the social and historical life of humankind that the natural will and the rational will are sometimes in close interrelationship, sometimes partly juxtaposed, and sometimes in opposition.

3. Just as the natural will of individuals transforms into rational will and conceptual thinking, which tends to overpower and eradicate its precursor, the initial collective forms of *Gemeinschaft* transform into *Gesellschaft*, with its rational will. This has characterized the course of

history, in which the civilization that supports the apparatus of the state has evolved out of folk culture.

This process and its major characteristics can be described as follows. The initial, dominating power in a region is the anonymous mass of people, who create the households, villages, and country towns. From among them there arise powerful, personally motivated individuals of many different types, including princes, feudal lords, and knights, as well as priests, artists, and scholars. To the extent they exist in a society where the people as a whole still largely control economic conditions, they are still controlled, to a greater or lesser degree, by the authority and will of the people. The ability of the newly arisen, exceptional individuals to organize at the national level, which is necessary if they are to become the dominant group in society, itself depends on economic conditions. Their true and fundamental control is economic control, which the business class achieves before them, with them, and even partly in opposition to them, by organizing and dominating the nation's labor force. The business class achieves such economic control in various ways, the most significant being calculated capitalist production or large-scale industry. The merchant class creates the technical conditions that allow for both the national unification of unrelated individuals and capitalistic production. By virtue of its nature and, especially, its origin, this class is international, national, and urban, that is, it belongs to *Gesellschaft*, not *Gemeinschaft*. In time, all traditional social groups and notable people, if not the entire folk populace, following the general tendency, take on the characteristics of the *Gesellschaft*.

In different places and under different conditions of everyday life people's dispositions change, and they approach life more hurriedly due to restless striving. This revolution in the social order results, at the same time, in a gradual change in both the substance and form of the law. In essence, the entire system becomes based on the contract, and the rational will that derives from the interests of *Gesellschaft* merges with the authoritative structure of the state to create, sustain, and transform the legal system. Following from this, the legal system can totally alter the *Gesellschaft* to promote its own interests and purposes, in accordance with the values of utility and effectiveness. The state becomes increasingly autonomous as it frees itself from acting in accordance with age-old traditions and customs and belief in their significance. In this way, the legal system transforms from its origins in the folkways, customs, and mores of society into a system that is the purely legalistic and derives from policy. At the same time, the many and diverse fellowships, communities, and commonwealths that emerged organically in society are replaced by the state, its departments, and individuals. Along with this transformation, the characteristics of the people that were shaped by the traditional, now defunct, culture and institutions also change to adapt to new, capricious laws and policies. The traditional institutions, without the support that customs, religion and conviction in their truth gave to them, no longer can retain their firm grip on the people.

Finally the intellectual life of the people undergoes a complete transformation, which both results from and affects the foregoing changes. Once formerly ingrained totally in the imagination, intellectual life now becomes dependent on thinking. Whereas previously it was dominated by belief in invisible beings, spirits, and gods, now it focuses on scrutiny of the visible world. Religion, which derives from custom and tradition, necessarily yields supremacy to science, which is a product of conscious thinking that results from education, and thus is far removed from the mass of the ordinary people. Religion is inherently and immediately moral, by its very nature, because it expresses most deeply the physical-spiritual link that binds different generations together. In contrast, science derives any moral significance it may have only from its ability to observe the laws of human society, and it creates arbitrary rules, which result in a reasonable and orderly form of social organization. Religion increasingly loses, and science increasingly gains, the ability to influence the mental life of individuals. We will now turn our attention to the great contrasts involved in the opposite poles of this dichotomy and their variations, using research findings from earlier, hard working generations. By way of introduction, however, the following few brief remarks may serve to simplify the fundamental principles.

4. We have designated the exterior types of community life that are represented by natural will and *Gemeinschaft* as house, village, and town, which are genuine and continuing types of historical life. The people lived together in these ways even in the earlier and middle stages of a developed *Gesellschaft*. Among those types, the town is paramount, that is, it represents the most complex form of social life. It shares local characteristics with the village, but differs sharply from the house, with its family-dominated characteristics. Both the village and the town preserve many characteristics of the family, but the village preserves more than the town. These characteristics almost totally disappear when the town develops into the city. Then both individuals and families become

separated, and their once shared environment becomes merely a place to live, either by accident or purposeful choice. Just as the town coexists within the larger city to some extent, we also find that elements of *Gemeinschaft* life, which is the only genuine form of life, persist within the *Gesellschaft*, even though they are in a process of decay. The more the characteristics of *Gesellschaft* spread throughout a nation or group of nations and become established, on the other hand, the more this entire "country" or "world" comes to look like one huge city. Nonetheless, in the city and wherever the general conditions that define the *Gesellschaft* predominate, the only people who are active and alive are the wealthy and the cultured among the upper strata. The lower strata attempt to conform to their standards, in part to supplant them and in part to imitate them, as a way to attain social power and freedom for themselves. For both groups the city, (as for the "nation" and the "world"), consists of free individuals who engage in acts of exchange and cooperate with each other, without any *Gemeinschaft* elements developing among them, except intermittently or as a holdover from prior conditions. The opposite is actually the case, because the many external contacts, contracts, and contractual relationship serve only to disguise the abundant inner hostilities and antagonistic interests that exist. The latter is especially true for the antagonism between the rich, or the so-called cultured, class and the poor, or the servant class, who attempt to hinder and destroy each other. This antagonism gives the "city" its dual character, according to Plato, and causes it to be divided from within. It also is what defines the nature of a city, according to our theory, and such antagonism exists within every large-scale relationship between capital and labor. Ordinary town life continues within the sphere of the *Gemeinschaft* of family and rural life, dedicated to certain agricultural activities, but primarily concerned with the art and craft that emerge from those natural needs and habits. City life is very different, however, because there the town-based activities merely serve as the means and tools for the unique purposes of the city.

The city generally typifies *Gesellschaft*. It is basically a commercial center, and to the degree that commerce dominates its productive labor, it is also a factory center. Its wealth is capital, which is used in the various forms of trade, monetary, and industrial capital to multiply the wealth. Capital is a means for either appropriating the products of labor or profiting from the work of labor. The city also is the center of science and culture, which inevitably accompany commerce and industry. Artists must earn a living from their art within the exploitive capitalistic system. Ideas disseminate and change with amazing speed. Through mass distribution, speeches and books can become ways to significantly stimulate and influence others.

The city should not be confused with the national capital, which as the residence of the court and center of government displays many features of the city, but it has yet to reach that stage by virtue of the characteristics of its population and other conditions. In time, however, the utmost form of this kind is realized by the synthesis of the city and the national capital: the metropolis. More than being the essence of a national *Gesellschaft*, the metropolis comprises people from many diverse nations, i.e., from the world. Money and capital are limitless and omnipotent in the metropolis. It can produce and supply goods and scientific discoveries for the entire world, as well as create laws and shape public opinion for all nations. It symbolizes world markets and commerce, and in it world industries are concentrated. Its newspapers are global, and its people are drawn there from every corner of the earth out of curiosity and hunger for money and pleasure.

Thorstein Veblen

1857-1929

Source: *The Theory of the Leisure Class* (1918 edition)
Selection: Chapter IV: Conspicuous Consumption, pp. 68-88

A Norwegian-American sociologist and economist, Veblen undertook graduate work at Johns Hopkins University under Charles Sanders Peirce, the founder of the pragmatist school in philosophy, and subsequently received his Ph.D. in 1884 at Yale University, under the direction of William Graham Sumner, a proponent of laissez-faire economic policies. Perhaps the most important intellectual influences on Veblen were Charles Darwin and Herbert Spencer, whose work in the last half of the nineteenth century sparked an enormous interest in the evolutionary perspective on human societies. In 1892, Veblen became a professor at the newly opened University of Chicago, simultaneously serving as managing editor of the Journal of Political Economy. *In 1919, he helped found the New School for Social Research (today known as The New School), along with Charles Beard, James Robinson and John Dewey. His most famous book,* The Theory of the Leisure Class, *published in 1899, established him as an important social critic and introduced the term for which he is perhaps known more than any other, "conspicuous consumption." In the writing below, Veblen brilliantly and sardonically analyzes conspicuous consumption for different historical periods and cultures, and emphasizes the role it plays in defining relationships between individuals, families, and social classes.*

*

In what has been said of the evolution of the vicarious leisure class and its differentiation from the general body of the working classes, reference has been made to a further division of labour,—that between different servant classes. One portion of the servant class, chiefly those persons whose occupation is vicarious leisure, come to undertake a new, subsidiary range of duties—the vicarious consumption of goods. The most obvious form in which this consumption occurs is seen in the wearing of liveries and the occupation of spacious servants' quarters. Another, scarcely less obtrusive or less effective form of vicarious consumption, and a much more widely prevalent one, is the consumption of food, clothing, dwelling, and furniture by the lady and the rest of the domestic establishment.

But already at a point in economic evolution far antedating the emergence of the lady, specialised consumption of goods as an evidence of pecuniary strength had begun to work out in a more or less elaborate system. The beginning of a differentiation in consumption even antedates the appearance of anything that can fairly be called pecuniary strength. It is traceable back to the initial phase of predatory culture, and there is even a suggestion that an incipient differentiation in this respect lies back of the beginnings of the predatory life. This most primitive differentiation in the consumption of goods is like the later differentiation with which we are all so intimately familiar, in that it is largely of a ceremonial character, but unlike the latter it does not rest on a difference in accumulated wealth. The utility of consumption as an evidence of wealth is to be classed as a derivative growth. It is an adaptation to a new end, by a selective process, of a distinction previously existing and well established in men's habits of thought.

In the earlier phases of the predatory culture the only economic differentiation is a broad distinction between an honourable superior class made up of the able bodied men on the one side, and a base inferior class of labouring women on the other. According to the ideal scheme of life in force at that time it is the office of the men to consume what the women produce. Such consumption as falls to the women is merely incidental to their work; it is a means to their continued labour, and not a consumption directed to their own comfort and fullness of life. Unproductive consumption of goods is honourable, primarily as a mark of prowess and a perquisite of human dignity; secondarily it becomes substantially honourable in itself, especially the consumption of the more desirable things. The consumption of choice articles of food, and frequently also of rare articles of adornment, becomes tabu to the women and children; and if there is a base (servile) class of men, the tabu holds also for them. With a further advance in culture this tabu may change into simple custom of a more or less rigorous character; but whatever be the theoretical basis of the distinction which is maintained, whether it be a tabu or a larger conventionality, the features of the conventional scheme of consumption do not change easily. When the quasi-peaceable stage of industry is reached, with its fundamental institution of chattel slavery, the general principle, more or less rigorously applied, is that the base, industrious class should consume only what may be necessary to their subsistence. In the nature of things, luxuries and the comforts of life belong to the leisure class. Under the tabu, certain victuals, and more particularly certain beverages, are strictly reserved for the use of the superior class.

The ceremonial differentiation of the dietary is best seen in the use of intoxicating beverages and narcotics. If these articles of consumption are costly, they are felt to be noble and honorific. Therefore the base classes, primarily the women, practise an enforced continence with respect to these stimulants, except in countries where they are obtainable at a very low cost. From archaic times down through all the length of the patriarchal régime it has been the office of the women to prepare and administer these luxuries, and it has been the perquisite of the men of gentle birth and breeding to consume them. Drunkenness and the other pathological consequences of the free use of stimulants therefore tend in their turn to become honorific, as being a mark, at the second remove, of the superior status of those who are able to afford the indulgence. Infirmities induced by over-indulgence are among some peoples freely recognised as manly attributes. It has even happened that the name for certain diseased conditions of the body arising from such an origin has passed into everyday speech as a synonym for "noble" or "gentle." It is only at a relatively early stage of culture that the symptoms of expensive vice are conventionally accepted as marks of a superior status, and so tend to become virtues and command the deference of the community; but the reputability that attaches to certain expensive vices long retains so much of its force as to appreciably lessen the disapprobation visited upon the men of the wealthy or noble class for any excessive indulgence. The same invidious distinction adds force to the current disapproval of any indulgence of this kind on the part of women, minors, and inferiors. This invidious traditional distinction has not lost its force even among the more advanced peoples of today. Where the example set by the leisure class retains its imperative force in the regulation of the conventionalities, it is observable that the women still in great measure practise the same traditional continence with regard to stimulants.

This characterisation of the greater continence in the use of stimulants practised by the women of the reputable classes may seem an excessive refinement of logic at the expense of common sense. But facts within easy reach of any one who cares to know them go to say that the greater abstinence of women is in some part due to an imperative conventionality; and this conventionality is, in a general way, strongest where the patriarchal tradition—the tradition that the woman is a chattel —has retained its hold in greatest vigour. In a sense which has been greatly qualified in scope and rigour, but which has by no means lost its meaning even yet, this tradition says that the woman, being a chattel, should consume only what is necessary to her sustenance,—except so far as her further consumption contributes to the comfort or the good repute of her master. The consumption of luxuries, in the true sense, is a consumption directed to the comfort of the consumer himself, and is, therefore, a mark of the master. Any such consumption by others can take place only on a basis of sufferance. In communities where the popular habits of thought have been profoundly shaped by the patriarchal tradition we may accordingly look for survivals of the tabu on luxuries at least to the extent of a conventional deprecation of their use by the unfree and dependent class. This is more particularly true as regards certain luxuries, the use of which by the dependent class would detract sensibly from the comfort or pleasure of their masters, or which are held to be of doubtful legitimacy on other grounds. In the apprehension of the great conservative middle class of Western civilisation the use of these various stimulants is obnoxious to at least one, if not both, of these objections; and it is a fact too significant to be passed over that it is precisely among these middle classes of the Germanic culture, with their strong surviving sense of the patriarchal proprieties, that the women are to the greatest extent subject to a qualified tabu on narcotics and alcoholic beverages. With many qualifications—with more qualifications as the patriarchal tradition has gradually weakened—the general rule is felt to be right and binding that women should consume only for the benefit of their masters. The objection of course presents itself that expenditure on women's dress and household paraphernalia is an obvious exception to this rule; but it will appear in the sequel that this exception is much more obvious than substantial.

During the earlier stages of economic development, consumption of goods without stint, especially consumption of the better grades of goods,—ideally all consumption in excess of the subsistence minimum, —pertains normally to the leisure class. This restriction tends to disappear, at least formally, after the later peaceable stage has been reached, with private ownership of goods and an industrial system based on wage labour or on the petty household economy. But during the earlier quasi-peaceable stage, when so many of the traditions through which the institution of a leisure class has affected the economic life of later times were taking form and consistency, this principle has had the force of a conventional law. It has served as the norm to which consumption has tended to conform, and any appreciable departure from it is to be regarded as an aberrant form, sure to be eliminated sooner or later in the further course of development.

The quasi-peaceable gentleman of leisure, then, not only consumes of the staff of life beyond the minimum required for subsistence and physical efficiency, but his consumption also undergoes a specialisation as regards the quality of the goods consumed. He consumes freely and of the best, in food, drink, narcotics, shelter, services, ornaments, apparel, weapons and accoutrements, amusements, amulets, and idols or divinities. In the process of gradual amelioration which takes place in the articles of his consumption, the motive principle and the proximate aim of innovation is no doubt the higher efficiency of the improved and more elaborate products for personal comfort and well-being. But that does not remain the sole purpose of their consumption. The canon of reputability is at hand and seizes upon such innovations as are, according to its standard, fit to survive. Since the consumption of these more excellent goods is an evidence of wealth, it becomes honorific; and conversely, the failure to consume in due quantity and quality becomes a mark of inferiority and demerit.

This growth of punctilious discrimination as to qualitative excellence in eating, drinking, etc., presently affects not only the manner of life, but also the training and intellectual activity of the gentleman of leisure. He is no longer simply the successful, aggressive male,—the man of strength, resource, and intrepidity. In order to avoid stultification he must also cultivate his tastes, for it now becomes incumbent on him to discriminate with some nicety between the noble and the ignoble in consumable goods. He becomes a connoisseur in creditable viands of various degrees of merit, in manly beverages and trinkets, in seemly apparel and architecture, in weapons, games, dancers, and the narcotics. This cultivation of the aesthetic faculty requires time and application, and the demands made upon the gentleman in this direction therefore tend to change his life of leisure into a more or less arduous application to the business of learning how to live a life of ostensible leisure in a becoming way. Closely related to the requirement that the gentleman must consume freely and of the right kind of goods, there is the requirement that he must know how to consume them in a seemly manner. His life of leisure must be conducted in due form. Hence arise good manners in the way pointed out in an earlier chapter. High-bred manners and ways of living are items of conformity to the norm of conspicuous leisure and conspicuous consumption.

Conspicuous consumption of valuable goods is a means of reputability to the gentleman of leisure. As wealth accumulates on his hands, his own unaided effort will not avail to sufficiently put his opulence in evidence by this method. The aid of friends and competitors is therefore brought in by resorting to the giving of valuable presents and expensive feasts and entertainments. Presents and feasts had probably another origin than that of naive ostentation, but they acquired their utility for this purpose very early, and they have retained that character to the present; so that their utility in this respect has now long been the substantial ground on which these usages rest. Costly entertainments, such as the potlatch or the ball, are peculiarly adapted to serve this end. The competitor with whom the entertainer wishes to institute a comparison is, by this method, made to serve as a means to the end. He consumes vicariously for his host at the same time that he is a witness to the consumption of that excess of good things which his host is unable to dispose of single-handed, and he is also made to witness his host's facility in etiquette.

In the giving of costly entertainments, other motives, of a more genial kind, are of course also present. The custom of festive gatherings probably originated in motives of conviviality and religion; these motives are also present in the later development, but they do not continue to be the sole motives. The latter-day leisure-class festivities and entertainments may continue in some slight degree to serve the religious need and in a higher degree the needs of recreation and conviviality, but they also serve an invidious purpose; and they serve it none the less effectually for having a colourable non-invidious ground in these more avowable motives. But the economic effect of these social amenities is not therefore lessened, either in the vicarious consumption of goods or in the exhibition of difficult and costly achievements in etiquette.

As wealth accumulates, the leisure class develops further in function and structure, and there arises a differentiation within the class. There is a more or less elaborate system of rank and grades. This differentiation is furthered by the inheritance of wealth and the consequent inheritance of gentility. With the inheritance of gentility goes the inheritance of obligatory leisure; and gentility of a sufficient potency to entail a life of leisure may be inherited without the complement of wealth required to maintain a dignified leisure. Gentle blood may be transmitted without goods enough to afford a reputably free consumption at one's ease. Hence results a class of impecunious gentlemen of leisure, incidentally referred to already. These half-caste gentlemen of leisure fall into a system of hierarchical gradations. Those who stand near the higher and the highest grades of the wealthy leisure class, in point of birth, or in point of wealth, or both, outrank the remoter-born and the pecuniarily weaker. These lower grades, especially the impecunious, or marginal, gentlemen of leisure, affiliate themselves by a system of dependence or fealty to the great ones; by so doing they gain an increment of repute, or of the means with which to lead a life of leisure, from their patron. They become his courtiers or retainers, servants; and being fed and countenanced by their patron they are indices of his rank and vicarious consumers of his superfluous wealth. Many of these affiliated gentlemen of leisure are at the same time lesser men of substance in their own right; so that some of them are scarcely at all, others only partially, to be rated as vicarious consumers. So many of them, however, as make up the retainers and hangers-on of the patron may be classed as vicarious consumers without qualification. Many of these again, and also many of the other aristocracy of less degree, have in turn attached to their persons a more or less comprehensive group of vicarious consumers in the persons of their wives and children, their servants, retainers, etc.

Throughout this graduated scheme of vicarious leisure and vicarious consumption the rule holds that these offices must be performed in some such manner, or under some such circumstance or insignia, as shall point plainly to the master to whom this leisure or consumption pertains, and to whom therefore the resulting increment of good repute of right inures. The consumption and leisure executed by these persons for their master or patron represents an investment on his part with a view to an increase of good fame. As regards feasts and largesses this is obvious enough, and the imputation of repute to the host or patron here takes place immediately, on the ground of common notoriety. Where leisure and consumption is performed vicariously by henchmen and retainers, imputation of the resulting repute to the patron is effected by their residing near his person so that it may be plain to all men from what source they draw. As the group whose good esteem is to be secured in this way grows larger, more patent means are required to indicate the imputation of merit for the leisure performed, and to this end uniforms, badges, and liveries come into vogue. The wearing of uniforms or liveries implies a considerable degree of dependence, and may even be said to be a mark of servitude, real or ostensible. The wearers of uniforms and liveries may be roughly divided into two classes—the free and the servile, or the noble and the ignoble. The services performed by them are likewise divisible into noble and ignoble. Of course the distinction is not observed with strict consistency in practice; the less debasing of the base services and the less honorific of the noble functions are not infrequently merged in the same person. But the general distinction is not on that account to be overlooked. What may add some perplexity is the fact that this fundamental distinction between noble and ignoble, which rests on the nature of the ostensible service performed, is traversed by a secondary distinction into honorific and humiliating, resting on the rank of the person for whom the service is performed or whose livery is worn. So, those offices which are by right the proper employment of the leisure class are noble; such are government, fighting, hunting, the care of arms and accoutrements, and the like,—in short, those which may be classed as ostensibly predatory employments. On the other hand, those employments which properly fall to the industrious class are ignoble; such as handicraft or other productive labour, menial services, and the like. But a base service performed for a person of very high degree may become a very honorific office; as for instance the office of a Maid of Honour or of a Lady in Waiting to the Queen, or the King's Master of the Horse or his Keeper of the Hounds. The two offices last named suggest a principle of some general bearing. Whenever, as in these cases, the menial service in question has to do directly with the primary leisure employments of fighting and hunting, it easily acquires a reflected honorific character. In this way great honour may come to attach to an employment which in its own nature belongs to the baser sort. [. . .]

With the disappearance of servitude, the number of vicarious consumers attached to any one gentleman tends, on the whole, to decrease. The like is of course true, and perhaps in a still higher degree, of the number of dependents who perform vicarious leisure for him. In a general way, though not wholly nor consistently, these two groups coincide. The dependent who was first delegated for these duties was the wife, or the chief wife; and, as would be expected, in the later development of the institution, when the number of persons by whom these duties are customarily performed gradually narrows, the wife remains the last. In the higher grades of society a large volume of both these kinds of service is required; and here the wife is of course still assisted in the work by a more or less numerous corps of menials. But as we descend the social scale, the point is presently reached where the duties of vicarious leisure and consumption devolve upon the wife alone. In the communities of the Western culture, this point is at present found among the lower middle class.

And here occurs a curious inversion. It is a fact of common observation that in this lower middle class there is no pretence of leisure on the part of the head of the household. Through force of circumstances it has fallen into disuse. But the middle-class wife still carries on the business of vicarious leisure, for the good name of the household and its master. In descending the social scale in any modern industrial community, the primary fact—the conspicuous leisure of the master of the household—disappears at a relatively high point. The head of the middle-class household has been reduced by economic circumstances to turn his hand to gaining a livelihood by occupations which often partake largely of the character of industry, as in the case of the ordinary business man of to-day. But the derivative fact—the vicarious leisure and consumption rendered by the wife, and the auxiliary vicarious performance of leisure by menials—remains in vogue as a conventionality which the demands of reputability will not suffer to be slighted. It is by no means an uncommon spectacle to find a man applying himself to work with the utmost assiduity, in order that his wife may in due form render for him that degree of vicarious leisure which the common sense of the time demands.

The leisure rendered by the wife in such cases is, of course, not a simple manifestation of idleness or indolence. It almost invariably occurs disguised under some form of work or household duties or social amenities, which prove on analysis to serve little or no ulterior end beyond showing that she does not and need not occupy herself with anything that is gainful or that is of substantial use. As has already been noticed under the head of manners, the greater part of the customary round of domestic cares to which the middle-class housewife gives her time and effort is of this character. Not that the results of her attention to household matters, of a decorative and mundificatory character, are not pleasing to the sense of men trained in middle-class proprieties; but the taste to which these effects of household adornment and tidiness appeal is a taste which has been formed under the selective guidance of a canon of propriety that demands just these evidences of wasted effort. The effects are pleasing to us chiefly because we have been taught to find them pleasing. There goes into these domestic duties much solicitude for a proper combination of form and colour, and for other ends that are to be classed as aesthetic in the proper sense of the term; and it is not denied that effects having some substantial aesthetic value are sometimes attained. Pretty much all that is here insisted on is that, as regards these amenities of life, the housewife's efforts are under the guidance of traditions that have been shaped by the law of conspicuously wasteful expenditure of time and substance. If beauty or comfort is achieved,—and it is a more or less fortuitous circumstance if they are,—they must be achieved by means and methods that commend themselves to the great economic law of wasted effort. The more reputable, "presentable" portion of middle-class household paraphernalia are, on the one hand, items of conspicuous consumption, and on the other hand, apparatus for putting in evidence the vicarious leisure rendered by the housewife.

The requirement of vicarious consumption at the hands of the wife continues in force even at a lower point in the pecuniary scale than the requirement of vicarious leisure. At a point below which little if any pretence of wasted effort, in ceremonial cleanness and the like, is observable, and where there is assuredly no conscious attempt at ostensible leisure, decency still requires the wife to consume some goods conspicuously for the reputability of the household and its head. So that, as the latter-day outcome of this evolution of an archaic institution, the wife, who was at the outset the drudge and chattel of the man, both in fact and in theory,—the producer of goods for him to consume,—has become the ceremonial consumer of goods which he produces. But she still quite unmistakably remains his chattel in theory; for the habitual rendering of vicarious leisure and consumption is the abiding mark of the un-free servant.

This vicarious consumption practised by the house-hold of the middle and lower classes can not be counted as a direct expression of the leisure-class scheme of life, since the household of this pecuniary grade does not belong within the leisure class. It is rather that the leisure-class scheme of life here comes to an expression at the second remove. The leisure class stands at the head of the social structure in point of reputability; and its manner of life and its standards of worth therefore afford the norm of reputability for the community. The observance of these standards, in some degree of approximation, becomes incumbent upon all classes lower in the scale. In modern civilized communities the lines of demarcation between social classes have grown vague and transient, and wherever this happens the norm of reputability imposed by the upper class extends its coercive influence with but slight hindrance down through the social structure to the lowest strata. The result is that the members of each stratum accept as their ideal of decency the scheme of life in vogue in the next higher stratum, and bend their energies to live up to that ideal. On pain of forfeiting their good name and their self-respect in case of failure, they must conform to the accepted code, at least in appearance.

The basis on which good repute in any highly organised industrial community ultimately rests is pecuniary strength; and the means of showing pecuniary strength, and so of gaining or retaining a good name, are leisure and a conspicuous consumption of goods. Accordingly, both of these methods are in vogue as far down the scale as it remains possible; and in the lower strata in which the two methods are employed, both offices are in great part delegated to the wife and children of the household. Lower still, where any degree of leisure, even ostensible, has become impracticable for the wife, the conspicuous consumption of goods remains and is carried on by the wife and children. The man of the household also can do something in this direction, and, indeed, he commonly does; but with a still lower descent into the levels of indigence—along the margin of the slums—the man, and presently also the children, virtually cease to consume valuable goods for appearances, and the woman remains virtually the sole exponent of the household's pecuniary decency. No class of society, not even the most abjectly poor, foregoes all customary conspicuous consumption. The last items of this category of consumption are not given up except under stress of the direst necessity. Very much of squalor and discomfort will be endured before the last trinket or the last pretence of pecuniary decency is put away. There is no class and no country that has yielded so abjectly before the pressure of physical want as to deny themselves all gratification of this higher or spiritual need.

From the foregoing survey of the growth of conspicuous leisure and consumption, it appears that the utility of both alike for the purposes of reputability lies in the element of waste that is common to both. In the one case it is a waste of time and effort, in the other it is a waste of goods. Both are methods of demonstrating the possession of wealth, and the two are conventionally accepted as equivalents. The choice between them is a question of advertising expediency simply, except so far as it may be affected by other standards of propriety, springing from a different source. On grounds of expediency the preference may be given to the one or the other at different stages of the economic development. The question is, which of the two methods will most effectively reach the persons whose convictions it is desired to affect. Usage has answered this question in different ways under different circumstances.

So long as the community or social group is small enough and compact enough to be effectually reached by common notoriety alone,—that is to say, so long as the human environment to which the individual is required to adapt himself in respect of reputability is comprised within his sphere of personal acquaintance and neighbourhood gossip,—so long the one method is about as effective as the other. Each will therefore serve about equally well during the earlier stages of social growth. But when the differentiation has gone farther and it becomes necessary to reach a wider human environment, consumption begins to hold over leisure as an ordinary means of decency. This is especially true during the later, peaceable economic stage. The means of communication and the mobility of the population now expose the individual to the observation of many persons who have no other means of judging of his reputability than the display of goods (and perhaps of breeding) which he is able to make while he is under their direct observation.

The modern organisation of industry works in the same direction also by another line. The exigencies of the modern industrial system frequently place individuals and households in juxtaposition between whom there is little contact in any other sense than that of juxtaposition. One's neighbours, mechanically speaking, often are socially not one's neighbours, or even acquaintances; and still their transient good opinion has a high degree of utility. The only practicable means of impressing one's pecuniary ability on these unsympathetic observers of one's everyday life is an unremitting demonstration of ability to pay. In the modern community there is also a more frequent attendance at large gatherings of people to whom one's everyday life is unknown; in such places as churches, theatres, ballrooms, hotels, parks, shops, and the like. In order to impress these transient observers, and to retain one's self-complacency under their observation, the signature of one's pecuniary strength should be written in characters which he who runs may read. It is evident, therefore, that the present trend of the development is in the direction of heightening the utility of conspicuous consumption as compared with leisure.

It is also noticeable that the serviceability of consumption as a means of repute, as well as the insistence on it as an element of decency, is at its best in those portions of the community where the human contact of the individual is widest and the mobility of the population is greatest. Conspicuous consumption claims a relatively larger portion of the income of the urban than of the rural population, and the claim is also more imperative. The result is that, in order to keep up a decent appearance, the former habitually live hand-to-mouth to a greater extent than the latter. So it comes, for instance, that the American farmer and his wife and daughters are notoriously less modish in their dress, as well as less urbane in their manners, than the city artisan's family with an equal income. It is not that the city population is by nature much more eager for the peculiar complacency that comes of a conspicuous consumption, nor has the rural population less regard for pecuniary decency. But the provocation to this line of evidence, as well as its transient effectiveness, are more decided in the city. This method is therefore more readily resorted to, and in the struggle to outdo one another the city population push their normal standard of conspicuous consumption to a higher point, with the result that a relatively greater expenditure in this direction is required to indicate a given degree of pecuniary decency in the city. The requirement of conformity to this higher conventional standard becomes mandatory.

Émile Durkheim

1858-1917

Source: *The Rules of Sociological Method* (1912 edition)
Selection: Chapter I: What Is a Social Fact?, pp. 5-19

The French sociologist Émile Durkheim is considered one of the three founders of sociology as an academic discipline, along with Karl Marx and Max Weber. He is often described as a "positivist"—because he developed the sociological positivism of Auguste Comte in greater detail—and considered a precursor to "functionalism," along with Herbert Spencer. Durkheim is best known for his writings on social science methodology and brilliant sociological theories, which often incorporated empirical research and included the use of statistical techniques to analyze data. During his lifetime, he published numerous articles and books, including The Division of Labor in Society *(1893),* The Rules of Sociological Method *(1895),* Suicide *(1897), and* The Elementary Forms of Religious Life *(1912). He also founded the first European department of sociology at the University of Bordeaux, and in 1898 he founded the journal* L'Année Sociologique, *to publish and publicize the work of a growing number of his students and collaborators. In general, Durkheim was primarily concerned with how societies could maintain their integrity and coherence, i.e., their "solidarity," in the modern era, when traditional institutions and group identities were undergoing rapid change and fragmentation. According to many of his devotees, however, Durkheim's most important contribution to sociology was his insistence that sociology has a unique subject matter, different from all the physical sciences and psychology, which he called "social facts." In Chapter I of* The Rules of Sociological Method, *presented below*, Durkheim provides his classic discussion of this fundamental concept.

*

Prior to seeking the appropriate method for the study of social facts, it is important to know what facts may be called "social."

The question is especially necessary because precision is lacking in use of this term. It is commonly used to refer to virtually all phenomena that exist within society, even if they represent little social interest regarding some generality. According to this account, however, there is no human occurrence that cannot be termed social. Each individual drinks, sleeps, eats, and reasons, and society has a vital interest in seeing that these functions are exercised regularly. If, therefore, these facts were social, then sociology would not even have its own subject matter, and its subject matter would be confused with biology and psychology.

But in reality, in every society there is a group of phenomena that is clearly determined and separable, because they possess characteristics distinct from those that compose other natural sciences.

When I carry out my obligations as a sibling, spouse, or citizen, and honor commitments into which I have entered, I perform duties that are external to myself and my actions, and are defined by law and in custom. Even if they are in agreement with my own feelings, and reflect my inward sense of reality, they are still objective, because I did not prescribe those duties; I have received them through education. In addition, it often happens that we do not know the details of the obligations we assume, and to know them we have to refer to the legal code and its authoritative interpreters! Similarly, beliefs and practices of religious life are instilled in the individual from birth; if they existed before him, then it follows that they must exist outside of him. The system of signs I use to express my thoughts, the currency system I use to pay my debts, the credit instruments I use in my commercial relations, the practices I follow in my profession, etc., work independently of the purposes to which I put them. If one considers each individual in society, the preceding observations can apply to all of them. So there are ways of acting, thinking, and feeling that possess the remarkable characteristic that they exist outside of the individual's consciousness.

Not only are these types of conduct or thought external to the individual, but they are endowed with an imperative and coercive power whereby they impress themselves upon him, whether he likes it or not. No doubt, when I comply with them of my own volition, I feel this coercion little, if at all, as it is unnecessary. This characteristic is, nonetheless, an intrinsic nature of these facts; and the evidence is that I feel their imposition as soon as I try to resist. If I try to violate the rules of law, they react against me to prevent my action, given that there is enough time. Or they cancel my action and make it return to its normal form, if it has already been done but is possible to be reversed; or they make me pay the penalty for it, if it is not repairable. If rules that are purely moral are involved, then the conscience of the public curtails any act of offense by the surveillance it carries out over the conduct of citizens and the special sanctions it can readily employ. The control is less violent in other cases; it does not cease to exist, however. If I do not submit to society's conventions, if I dress in a way that is at odds with what is conventional in my country and in my class, then the laughter this will cause, the social avoidance I will incur, will produce the effect of a real punishment itself, albeit in a manner more attenuated. The constraint may be indirect in other cases, but no less effective. No one forces me to speak the language of my compatriots or to use the legal currencies, but it is impossible for me to do otherwise. If I was trying to avoid such necessity, my attempt would fail miserably. I am not prohibited, as an industrialist, from working with processes and methods of the last century; but if I do, I will certainly be ruined. Even when I am able to escape these rules and violate them successfully, I must still fight against them. If I finally defeat them, I still significantly feel their constraining power due to the resistance they afford. There are no innovators, even lucky ones, who do not encounter in their undertakings such resistances.

We have an order of facts, therefore, with very special characteristics: they consist of ways of acting, thinking, and feeling that are external to the individual and possess powers of coercion by virtue of which they can exercise control over him. Thus, they cannot be confused with organic phenomena, since they include representations and actions, nor with the psychic phenomena, which exist only in and through individual consciousness. They therefore constitute a new species, and it is only to them that we can specifically apply the term social. It is suitable for them because it is clear that, not having the individual as their substratum, they can only have society, either political society as a whole or partial groups it includes—religious denominations, political and literary organizations, professional corporations, etc. Furthermore, this is as it should be for these groups alone, because the word "social" means identifying those phenomena that do not fit into any of the categories of facts already incorporated and named. They are, therefore, the exclusive field of sociology. It is true that this word "constraint," by which we define them, might anger zealous supporters of absolute individualism. Because they profess that the individual is perfectly autonomous, it seems to them that the individual is reduced every time he feels that he depends on something other than himself. Today, however, since no one doubts that we do not develop most of our ideas and trends, but rather that they come to us from the outside, the only way they can penetrate us is by imposing themselves upon us. That is the sole meaning of our definition. We know, moreover, that any social constraint does not necessarily exclude the individual personality.[1]

However, since the examples we just cited (legal and moral rules, religious dogmas, financial systems, etc.) refer to long-established beliefs and practices, it could be said, following the above, that a social fact can exist only when there is a well-defined social organization. There are other facts, however, without such crystallized forms that have the same objectivity and same ascendancy over the individual. They are what we call social "currents." In a public assembly, for example, the great feelings of enthusiasm, indignation, and pity brought forth do not reside in any particular person's consciousness. They come to each person assembled from the outside, and can affect all individuals despite themselves. If I abandon myself without reservation, I probably will not be aware of the pressure they exert over me, but as soon as I try to fight against them, I will be aware of such pressure. Should an individual attempt to oppose one of these collective expressions, the feelings he is rejecting will turn upon him. If this external, coercive power strikes at us so sharply during resistance, then it must exist, in the situations cited above, even though we are not conscious of it. We are thus fooled by an illusion that causes us to believe we have personally created what has been imposed on us from the outside. But if our willingness to go along with this belief hides the pressure upon us, it does not eliminate it. Thus air does not stop having weight just because we no longer feel the weight. Even when an individual has spontaneously experienced the common emotion, the impression experienced is totally different from what he would have felt if he were alone. Furthermore, once the assembly has disbanded and the social influences have ceased to act on us, and we find ourselves alone, we are apt to feel that the emotions we have experienced seem alien, and we have difficulty recognizing ourselves. We then realize we have received the emotions much more than we have created them. This experience can cause us to feel horror if it runs contrary to our nature. Thus perfectly harmless individuals can sometimes be moved to commit acts of atrocity when assembled in crowds. What we say about these transient outbursts also applies to more sustainable movements of opinion, which occur constantly around us, either throughout society or in more restricted circles, as regards matters that are religious, political, literary, artistic, etc.

Moreover, by a characteristic experience one can confirm this definition of a social fact, simply by observing how children are raised. When we look at the facts as they are and as they have always been, it is apparent that all education is a continuous effort to impose upon the child how to see, feel, and act in ways that would not have been arrived at spontaneously. Early in his life, we compel him to eat, drink, and sleep at regular times, and to be clean, quiet, and obedient; later, we require that he learns to take others into account, complies with customs and usage, works, etc. If, over time, he stops feeling this constraint, it is because, little by little, it has given birth to habits, to internal tendencies that make it unnecessary; but they have replaced the constraint only because they derive from it. It is true that, according to Mr. Spencer, a rational education should reject such processes and let the child freely do as he will. This pedagogical theory, however, has never been put into practice by any known people, and so it is only a personal desideratum and not a fact that can stand in opposition to the facts stated above. What makes the latter particularly instructive is the fact that education has precisely the goal of creating a person who is social. It therefore can be seen, although in an abbreviated way, how history has given rise to the social being. The continuous pressure that the child undergoes is the same pressure of the social environment that seeks to shape the child in its own image, and in which the parents and teachers are but representatives and intermediaries.

It is not, therefore, their generality that can be used to characterize sociological phenomena. Thoughts found in each individual's consciousness and movements that are repeated are thus not the explanation of social facts. If just this characteristic is used to define them, then it is done so wrongly, and they are being confused with what could be called their individual incarnations. Social facts are composed of the beliefs, tendencies, and practices of the group collectively. The forms that these collective states can take when they are refracted through individuals, however, are things of another type. What categorically demonstrates the nature of this duality is that these two orders of facts often occur in a detached state from each other. Indeed, some of these ways of acting or thinking acquire, as a result of repetition, a sort of consistency that separates them from one another, so to speak, and isolates them from the distinct events that reflect them. They take a shape, a concrete form unique to them, and constitute a reality *sui generis* that is very different from the individual facts that manifest the reality. Collective practice exists not only in the state of immanence in the successive acts that it determines, but also by a privilege for which we can find no example in the biological world, it expresses itself, at last, in a formula that is repeated by word of mouth, passed along by education, and even established in writing. This is the origin and nature of the aphorisms and popular sayings, legal and moral rules, articles of faith that embody the beliefs of religious or political sects, codes of taste established by literary schools, etc. None of these ways of behaving and thinking can be found to fully exist in applications made by individuals, since they can exist even without being currently applied.

Without doubt this dissociation does not always show itself with the same clarity. The simple fact that dissociation exists indisputably in the many and important cases cited, however, proves that the social fact is separate from its individual manifestations. Indeed, even when the dissociation is not immediately apparent to observation, this result can often be achieved through certain methodological procedures. It is necessary to carry out this approach if we are to be able to isolate the social fact from the amalgam and observe it in its state of purity. Thus, there are certain currents of opinion that exhibit an uneven intensity, depending on the time and country in which they exist, that thrust us, for example, towards marriage, suicide, a more or less high birth rate, etc. These currents are obviously social facts. At first, they seem inseparable from the shapes they take in individual cases. But statistics provide us with the means to isolate them. Indeed, they are not accurately reflected in the rates of births, marriage, suicides, i.e., by the number obtained by dividing the average annual total of weddings, births, and voluntary deaths by the number of persons old enough to marry, procreate, or commit suicide.[2] Because each of these statistics includes all particular cases without distinction, the individual circumstances that may have contributed to the production of the phenomenon neutralize each other and, as a result, do not contribute to the determination of the phenomenon. What it expresses is a definite state of the collective mind.

That is what social phenomena are when they are free of any foreign element. With regard to their private manifestations, they do exhibit something social, since they reproduce, in part, the collective model. Each manifestation also depends to a great degree, however, on the individual's psychic and organic constitution, and the special circumstances in which he is placed. They are, therefore, not strictly sociological phenomena. They conform to both domains simultaneously, so one could call them socio-psychological. They interest the sociologist even though they do not constitute the immediate material of sociology. We can see the same characteristic in the life forms of those mixed natural phenomena studied in combined sciences such as bio-chemistry.

One could argue that a phenomenon can be collective only if it is common to all members of society, or at the very least to most of them, and thus if it is general. No doubt, but if it is general it is because it is collective (i.e., more or less required); it is much further from being collective, however, because it is general. It is a state of the group that is repeated in individuals because it forces itself upon them. It exists in each part because it exists in the whole, but it does not exist so much in the whole because it exists in the parts. This is especially obvious with beliefs and practices transmitted to us from earlier generations. We receive them and adopt them because they are the work of the old, venerable collective. It is important to note that the vast majority of social phenomena come to us in this manner. But even when the social fact is due, in part, to our direct cooperation, it is not different in nature. An emotional display by individuals in an assembly does not simply express all that the separate individuals share in common, but is something other, as we have shown. It is a result of their shared life, a product of the actions and reactions between the minds of individuals. And if each of them hears its echo, it is precisely because of the special energy that comes from its collective origins. If all hearts vibrate in unison, it is not the result of a concordance that is spontaneous and preset; it is because a single force is thrusting them in the same direction. Each is led by all.

We have now reached the point where we can represent, in a precise way, the field of sociology. It includes only a specific group of phenomena. A social fact is known by the power of external coercion it exercises or that it is likely to exercise on individuals; and the presence of this power is known, in turn, by the existence of some established sanction, or by the resistance that the fact presents to any individual enterprise that tends to harm it. However, one can also define it by determining the scope of its existence within the group, provided that, following the previous remarks, one takes care to include a second and essential characteristic that exists independently of the individual forms that it may assume during the course of its dissemination throughout the group. This latter criterion, in some cases, is even easier to apply than the previous one. In effect, the constraint is easy to see when it is transmitted to the outside through any direct reaction by society, as in the case of law, morality, beliefs, practices, lifestyles. But when it is only indirect, like that carried out by an economic organization, it is sometimes less easy to see. The generality combined with objectivity can be easier to establish. Moreover, this second definition is but another form of the first; for if a way of acting, which is external to the consciousness of individuals, becomes generalized, it can only be so if it exerts force upon them.[3]

However, it could be asked if this definition is complete. Certainly the facts that we have provided as its basis exhibit all manner of being; they are of the order physiological. However there are also ways of collective being, that is to say, social facts of an anatomical or morphological order. Sociology is not able to dissociate itself from the concerns of the substratum of collective life. The number and nature of the basic parts that compose society, how they are arranged, the degree of coalescence they have arrived at, the distribution of the population on the surface of a territory, the number and nature of the communication routes, the designs of homes, etc., do not appear, at first sight, to be related to ways of acting, feeling, or thinking. First and foremost, however, these various phenomena have the same characteristics we used to define the others. They impose themselves on individuals the same as the ways of acting we have spoken of previously. Indeed, when one wants to learn the way that a society is divided politically, the composition of these divisions, and the extent of closeness that exists between them, it is not through material inspection and geographical observations that we can obtain this knowledge; because these divisions are social even though they have some basis in physical nature. We can study such political organization only through public law, because it is this law that determines its nature, just as it determines our domestic and civic relations. It is, therefore, no less compulsory. If the population gathers in our cities instead of being dispersed through the countryside, it is due to a current of opinion, a collective thrust, which imposes this concentration on individuals. We are no more able to choose the design of our homes than of our clothes; at the least, one is as obligatory as the other. The communication system compellingly determines the direction of internal migrations and trade, and also the intensity of such exchanges and migrations, etc., etc. Consequently, there would be, at best, a reason to add to the list of phenomena already listed one more category that has the distinctive mark of a social fact; and as that enumeration was not thoroughly exhaustive, this addition would not be indispensable.

But it is not even useful; because these ways of being are just ways that have been consolidated. The political structure of a society is only the way in which the different societal segments have gotten used to living with each other. Depending on how close their traditional relationships are, the segments will be more merged together or more confused. The type of housing that imposes itself on us is merely the way in which everyone around us and, in part, previous generations, have traditionally built their houses. The communication network is only the conduit that has been carved out by the regular current of trade and migrations, etc. No doubt, if morphological order phenomena were the only ones that displayed this type of fixation, it would seem as if they constituted a unique species. But a legal rule is an arrangement no less permanent than a type of architecture, and yet it is a physiological fact. A simple legal maxim is assuredly more malleable; but it has many forms more rigid than a simple professional custom or fashion. There is thus a continuous range of gradations that link structural facts to those free currents of social life that exist without a definite mould. The differences between them, therefore, are only the degree of consolidation they present. They both are life forms at different stages of crystallization. Without doubt, it would be beneficial to reserve the name morphological for social facts that concern the social substrate, but provided we do not lose sight that they are of the same nature as the others. Our definition will, therefore, include all that has to be defined, if we say: *a social fact is any way of acting, whether it is fixed or not, able to exercise an external constraint over the individual; or, which is general over the whole of a given society while at the same time having an existence of its own that is independent of its individual manifestations.*[4]

Notes

[1] This is not to say, of course, that all constraint is normal. We will return to this point later.

[2] One does not find suicide at every age, nor does suicide occur at every age of life with the same intensity.

[3] This definition of the social fact is very far removed, as can be seen, from the definition upon which Tarde's inventive system rests. First, we have to declare that our research has not led us to support the main influence Tarde attributes to imitation in the birth of collective facts. Even more, from his definition, which is not a theory but a simple summary of observed, given data, it seems well to conclude that imitation rarely if ever expresses what is fundamental and characteristic about social facts. Without doubt, every social fact is imitated and tends to become generalized, as we have shown, but that is because it is social, that is to say, compulsory. Its expansive capability is the consequence, not the cause, of its sociological character. If only social facts could produce this consequence, then imitation might serve to define them, even if it could not explain them. An individual state that impacts others, however, still remains individual. Moreover,

one may wonder if the term "imitation" is suitable to designate a propagation that results from a coercive influence. Under this novel term one finds that very different phenomena are confused that should be distinguished.

[4] This close resemblance of life and structure, organ and function, can easily be established in sociology, because between the two extremes there exists a series of intermediate stages that are immediately observable and show the connection between them. Biology does not have the same resource. It is justifiable to believe, however, that inductions on this subject from the former, sociology, are applicable to the latter, biology, and that, in organisms as in societies, only differences in degree exist between these two kinds of facts.

Georg Simmel

1858-1918

Source: *American Journal of Sociology* (1910-11)
Selection: How is Society Possible?, pp. 372-391

Simmel was a German sociologist and philosopher who did much to establish sociology as a basic social science in Germany during his lifetime, with more than 200 published articles and over a dozen published books in several social science fields. After obtaining his doctorate degree in 1881 from the University of Berlin with a dissertation on Kant, he remained at the university as an unpaid lecturer for 15 years, living on student fees and a substantial inheritance, where he taught courses in sociology as well as philosophy, history, ethics, and cultural criticism. He was also a cofounder of the German Society for Sociology, together with Ferdinand Tönnies and Max Weber. In many of his writings, Simmel focused on social and cultural phenomena in terms of "forms" and "contents" that existed in a transient relationship, with form becoming content and vice versa, depending on the context. He especially sought to isolate the general forms of social interaction from the specific content of definite kinds of activity, such as political, economic, social, and aesthetic activities. His neo-Kantian approach to social science laid the foundations for sociological antipositivism, asking "What is society?" in a direct allusion to Kant's question "What is nature?" This analysis may be seen in the following seminal writing titled "How Is Society Possible?"

*

Kant could propose and answer the fundamental question of his philosophy, How is nature possible?, only because for him nature was nothing but the representation (*Vorstellung*) of nature. This does not mean merely that "the world is my representation," that we thus can speak of nature only so far as it is a content of our consciousness, but that what we call nature is a special way in which our intellect assembles, orders, and forms the sense-perceptions. These "given" perceptions, of color, taste, tone, temperature, resistance, smell, which in the accidental sequence of subjective experience course through our consciousness, are in and of themselves not yet "nature;" but they become "nature" through the activity of the mind, which combines them into objects and series of objects, into substances and attributes and into causal coherences. [. . .] The question then, How is nature possible?, i.e., what are the conditions which must be present in order that a "nature" may be given, is resolved by him through discovery of the forms which constitute the essence of our intellect and therewith bring into being "nature" as such.

It is at once suggested that it is possible to treat in an analogous fashion the question of the aprioristic conditions on the basis of which society is possible. Here too individual elements are given which in a certain sense always remain in their discreteness, as is the case with the sense-perceptions, and they undergo their synthesis into the unity of a society only through a process of consciousness which puts the individual existence of the several elements into relationship with that of the others in definite forms and in accordance with definite laws. The decisive difference between the unity of a society and that of nature, however, is this: the latter—according to the Kantian standpoint here presupposed—comes to existence exclusively in the contemplating unity (Subject), it is produced exclusively by that mind upon and out of the sense materials which are not in themselves interconnected. On the contrary, the societary unity is realized by its elements without further mediation, and with no need of an observer, because these elements are consciously and synthetically active. The Kantian theorem, Connection (*Verbindung*) can never inhere in the things, since it is only brought into existence by the mind (Subject), is not true of the societary connection, which is rather immediately realized in the "things"—namely, in this case the individual souls. Moreover, this societary connection as synthesis, remains something purely psychical and without parallels with space-structures and their reactions. [. . .]

What forms must be at the basis, or what specific categories must we bring along, so to speak, in order that the consciousness may arise, and what consequently are the forms which the resulting consciousness—i.e., society as a fact of knowing—must bear? We may call this the epistemological theory of society. In what follows, I am trying to sketch certain of these a priori effective conditions or forms of socialization. These cannot, to be sure, like the Kantian categories, be designated by a single word. Moreover, I present them only as illustrations of the method of investigation.

1. The picture which one man gets of another from personal contact is determined by certain distortions which are not simple deceptions from incomplete experience, defective vision, sympathetic or antipathetic prejudice; they are rather changes in principle in the composition of the real object. These are, to begin with, of two dimensions. In the first place we

see the other party in some degree generalized. This may be because it is not within our power fully to represent in ourselves an individuality different from our own. Every reconstruction (*Nachbilden*) of a soul is determined by the similarity to it, and although this is by no means the only condition of psychical cognition—since on the one hand unlikeness seems at the same time requisite, in order to gain perspective and objectivity, on the other hand there is required an intellectual capacity which holds itself above likeness or unlikeness of being—yet complete cognition would nevertheless presuppose a complete likeness. It appears as though every man has in himself a deepest individuality-nucleus which cannot be subjectively reproduced by another whose deepest individuality is essentially different. And that this requirement is not logically compatible with that distance and objective judgment on which the representation of another otherwise rests, is proved by the mere fact that complete knowledge of the individuality of another is denied to us; and all interrelations of men with one another are limited by the varying degrees of this deficiency. Whatever its cause may be, its consequence at all events is a generalization of the psychical picture of the other person, a dissolving of the outlines, which adds to the singularity of this picture a relationship with others. We posit every man, with especial bearing upon our practical attitude toward him, as that type of man to which his individuality makes him belong. We think him, along with all his singularity, only under the universal category which does not fully cover him to be sure, and which he does not fully cover. This latter circumstance marks the contrast between this situation and that which exists between the universal idea and the particular which belongs under it. In order to recognize the man, we do not see him in his pure individuality, but carried, exalted or degraded by the general type under which we subsume him. Even when this transformation is so slight that we cannot immediately recognize it, or even if all the usual cardinal concepts of character fail us, such as moral or immoral, free or unfree, domineering or menial, etc.—in our own minds we designate the man according to an unnamed type with which his pure individuality does not precisely coincide.

Moreover this leads a step farther down. Precisely from the complete singularity of a personality we form a picture of it which is not identical with its reality, but still is not a general type. It is rather the picture which the person would present if he were, so to speak, entirely himself, if on the good or bad side he realized the possibility which is in every man. We are all fragments, not only of the universal man, but also of ourselves. We are onsets not merely of the type human being in general, not merely of the type good, bad, etc., but we are onsets of that not further in principle nameable individuality and singularity of our own selves which surrounds our perceptible actuality as though drawn with ideal lines. The vision of our neighbor, however, enlarges this fragment to that which we never are completely and wholly. He cannot see the fragments merely side by side as they are actually given, but as we offset the blind spot in our eye so that we are not conscious of it, in like manner we make of these fragmentary data the completeness of an individuality. The practice of life is more and more insistent that we shall form our picture of the man from the real details alone which we empirically know about him; but this very practice rests upon those changes and additions, upon the reconstruction of those given fragments into the generality of a type and into the completeness of this ideal personality.

This procedure, which is in principle attempted, although in reality it is seldom carried through to completeness, operates only within the already existing society as the apriori of the further reactions which develop between individuals. Within a sphere which has any sort of community of calling or of interests, every member looks upon every other, not in a purely empirical way, but on the basis of an apriori which this sphere imposes upon each consciousness which has part in it. In the circles of officers, of church members, of civil officials, of scholars, of members of families, each regards the other under the matter of course presupposition—this is a member of my group. From the common basis of life certain suppositions originate and people look upon one another through them as through a veil. This veil does not, to be sure, simply conceal the peculiarity of the individual, but it gives to this personality a new form, since its actual reality melts in this typical transformation into a composite picture. We see the other person not simply as an individual, but as colleague or comrade or fellow partisan; in a word, inhabitant of the same peculiar world; and this unavoidable, quite automatically operative presupposition is one of the means of bringing his personality and reality in the representation of another up to the quality and form demanded of his sociability (*Soziabilitat*).

The same is evidently true of members of different groups in their relations with one another. The plain citizen who makes the acquaintance of an officer cannot divest himself of the thought that this individual is an officer. And although this being an officer may belong to the given individuality, yet not in just the schematic way in which it prejudges his picture in the representation of the other person. The like is the case with the Protestant in contrast with the Catholic, the merchant with the official, the layman with the priest, etc. Everywhere there occur veilings of the outline of reality by the social generalization. This in principle prohibits discovery of that reality within a group which is in a high degree socially differentiated. Accordingly man's representation of man is thrown out of truth by dislocations, additions and subtractions from all these categories, which exert an a priori influence, since the generalization is always at the same time more or less than the individuality. That is, the individual is rated as in some particulars different from his actual self by the gloss imposed upon him when he is classified in a type, when he is compared with an imagined completeness of his own peculiarity, when he is credited with the characteristics of the social generality to which he belongs. Over and above all this there sways, as the principle of interpretation in cognition, the thought of his real solely individual equation; but since it appears as though determination of this equation would be the only way of arriving at the precisely founded relationship to the individual, as a matter of fact those changes and reshapings, which prevent this ideal recognition of him, are precisely the conditions through which the relationships which we know as the strictly social become possible—somewhat as with Kant the categories of reason, which form the immediately given into quite new objects, alone make the given world a knowable one.

2. Another category under which men (*Subjecte*) view themselves and one another, in order that, so formed, they may produce empirical society, may be formulated in the seemingly trivial theorem:—Each element of a group is not a societary part, but beyond that something else. This fact operates as social apriori in so far as the part of the individual which is not turned toward the group, or is not dissolved in it, does not lie simply without meaning by the side of his socially significant phase, is not a something external to the group, for which it *nolens volens* [i.e., [willing or not] affords space; but the fact that the individual, with respect to certain sides of his personality, is not an element of the group, constitutes the positive condition for the fact that he is such a group member in other aspects of his being. In other words, the sort of his socialized-being (*Vergesellschaftet-Seins*) is determined or partially determined by the sort of his not-socialized being. The analysis to follow will bring to light certain types whose sociological significance, even in their germ and nature, is fixed by the fact that they are in some way shut out

from the very group for which their existence is significant; for instance in the case of the stranger, the enemy, the criminal, and even the pauper. This applies, however, not merely in the case of such general characters, but in unnumbered modifications for every sort of individuality. That every moment finds us surrounded by relationships with human beings, and that the content of every moment's experience is directly or indirectly determined by these human beings, is no contradiction of the foregoing. On the contrary the social setting as such affects beings who are not completely bounded by it. For instance, we know that the civil official is not merely an official, the merchant not merely a merchant, the military officer not merely an officer. This extra-social being, his temperament and the deposit of his experiences, his interests and the worth of his personality, little as it may change the main matter of official, mercantile, military activities, gives the individual still, in every instance, for everyone with whom he is in contact, a definite shading, and it interpenetrates his social picture with extra-social imponderabilities. The whole commerce of men within the societary categories would be different, if each confronted the other only in that character which belongs to him in the role for which he is responsible in the particular category in which he appears at the moment. To be sure, individuals, like callings and social situations, are distinguished by the degree of that in-addition which they possess or admit along with their social content. The man in love or in friendship may be taken as marking the one pole of this series. In this situation, that which the individual reserves for himself, beyond those manifestations and activities which converge upon the other, in quantity approaches the zero point. Only a single life is present, which, so to speak, may be regarded or is lived from two sides: on the one hand from the inside, from the *terminus a quo* [i.e., a first point in time] of the active person; then on the other hand as the quite identical life, contemplated in the direction of the beloved person, under the category of *gis terminus ad quem* [i.e., a terminus or finishing point], which it completely adopts. With quite another tendency the Catholic priest presents in form the same phenomenon, in that his ecclesiastical function completely covers and swallows his being-for-himself. In the former of these extreme cases, the in-addition of the sociological activity disappears, because its content has completely passed over into consideration of the other party; in the second case, because the corresponding type of contents has, in principle, altogether disappeared. The opposite pole is exhibited by the phenomena of our modern civilization as they are determined by money economy. That is, man approaches the ideal of absolute objectivity as producer, or purchaser or seller, in a word as a performer of some economic function. Certain individuals in high places excepted, the individual life, the tone of the total personality, has disappeared from the function, the persons are merely the vehicles of an exchange of function and counterfunction occurring according to objective norms, and every thing which does not fit into this sheer thingness (*Sachlichkeit*) has also as a matter of fact disappeared from it. The in-addition has fully taken up into itself the personality with its special coloring, its irrationality, its inner life, and it has left to those societary activities only those energies, in pure abstraction, which specifically pertain to the activities.

Between these extremes the social individuals move in such a way that the energies and characteristics which are pointed toward the inner center always show a certain significance for the activities and inclinations which affect their associates. For, in the marginal case, even the consciousness that this social activity or attitude is something differentiated from the rest of the man, and does not enter into the sociological relationship along with that which he otherwise is and signifies—even this consciousness has quite positive influence upon the attitude which the subject assumes towards his fellows and they towards him. The apriori of the empirical social life is that the life is not entirely social. We form our interrelationships not alone under the negative reservation of a part of our personality which does not enter into them; this portion affects the social occurrences in the soul not alone through general psychological combinations, but precisely the formal fact that influence exerts itself outside of these determines the nature of this interworking.

Still further, one of the most important sociological formations rests on the fact that the societary structures are composed of beings who are at the same time inside and outside of them: namely that between a society and its individuals a relationship may exist like that between two parties—indeed that perhaps such relationship, open or latent, always exists. Therewith society produces perhaps the most conscious, at least universal conformation of a basic type of life in general: that the individual soul can never have a position within a combination outside of which it does not at the same time have a position, that it cannot be inserted into an order without finding itself at the same time in opposition to that order. This applies throughout the whole range from the most transcendental and universal interdependencies to the most singular and accidental.

The religious man feels himself completely encompassed by the divine being, as though he were merely a pulse-beat of the divine life; his own substance is unreservedly, and even in mystical identity, merged in that of the Absolute. And yet, in order to give this intermelting any meaning at all, the devotee must retain some sort of self existence, some sort of personal reaction, a detached ego, to which the resolution into the divine All-Being is an endless task, a process only, which would be neither metaphysically possible nor religiously feelable if it did not proceed from a self-being on the part of the person: the being one with God is conditional in its significance upon the being other than god. Beyond this converging toward the transcendental, the relationship to nature as a whole which the human mind manifests throughout its entire history shows the same form. On the one hand we know ourselves as articulated into nature, as one of its products, which stands alongside of every other as an equal among equals, as a point which nature's stuff and energies reach and leave, as they circle through running water and blossoming plants. And yet the soul has a feeling of a something self-existent (*eines Fursichseins*) which we designate with the logically so inexact concept freedom, offering an opposite (*ein Gegenuber und Paroli*) to all that energy an element of which we ever remain, which makes toward the radicalism which we may express in the formula, Nature is only a representation in the human soul. As, however, in this conception, nature with its undeniable peculiarity (*Eigengesetzlichkeit*) and hard reality is still subsumed under the concept of the ego, so on the other hand this ego, with all its freedom and self-containing (*Fursichsein*), with its juxtaposition to "mere nature," is still a member of nature. Precisely that is the overlapping natural correlation, that it embraces not one "mere nature," but also that being which is independent and often enough hostile to "mere nature," that this which according to the ego's deepest feeling of selfishness is external to the ego must still be the element of the ego. Moreover, this formula holds not less for the relationship between the individuals and the particular circles of their societary combinations; or if we generalize these combinations into the concept of societary-ness in the abstract, for the interrelation of individuals at large. We know ourselves on the one side as products of society. The physiological series of progenitors, their adaptations and fixations, the traditions of their labor, their knowledge and belief, of the whole spirit of the past crystallized in objective forms—all these determine the equipment and the contents of our life, so that the question might arise whether the individual is anything more than a receptacle in which previously existing elements mix in changing proportions; for although the elements were also in the last analysis produced by individuals, yet the contribution of each is a disappearing quantity, and only through their generic and societary merging were the factors produced in the synthesis of which in turn the ostensible individuality may consist. On the other hand we know ourselves as a member of society, woven with our life-process and its meaning and purpose quite as interdependently into its coexistence (*Nebeneinander*) as in the other view into its succession (*Nacheinander*). Little as we in our character as natural objects have a self-sufficiency, because the intersection of the natural elements proceeds through us as through completely selfless structures, and the equality before the laws of nature resolves our existence without remainder into a mere example of their necessity—quite as little do we live as societary beings around an autonomous center; but we are from moment to moment composed out of reciprocal relationships to others, and we are thus comparable with the corporeal substance which for us exists only as the sum of many impressions of the senses, but not as a self-sufficient entity. Now, however, we feel that this social diffusion does not completely dissolve our personality. This is not because of the reservations previously mentioned, or of particular contents whose meaning and development rest from the outset only in the individual soul, and finds no position at large in the social correlation. It is not only because of the molding of the social contents, whose unity as individual soul is not itself again of social nature, any more than the artistic form, in which the spots of color merge upon the canvas, can be derived from the chemical nature of the colors themselves. It is rather chiefly because the total life-content, however completely it may be applicable from the social antecedents and reciprocities, is yet at the same time capable of consideration under the category of the singular life, as experience of the individual and completely oriented with reference to this experience. The two, individual and experience, are merely different categories under which the same content falls, just as the same plant may be regarded now with reference to the biological conditions of its origin, again with reference to its practical utility, and still again with reference to its aesthetic meaning. The standpoint from which the existence of the individual may be correlated and understood may be assumed either within or without the individual; the totality of the life with all its socially derivable contents may be regarded as the centripetal destiny of its bearer, just as it still may pass, with all the parts reserved to the credit of the individual, as product and element of the social life.

Therewith, therefore, the fact of socialization brings the individual into the double situation from which I started: viz., that the individual has his setting in the socialization and at the same time is in antithesis with it, a member of its organism and at the same time a closed organic whole, an existence (*Sein*) for it and an existence for itself. The essential thing, however, and the meaning of the particular sociological apriori which has its basis herein, is this, that between individual and society the Within and Without are not two determinations which exist alongside of each other—although they may occasionally develop in that way, and even to the degree of reciprocal enmity—but that they signify the whole unitary position of the socially living human being. His existence is not merely, in subdivision of the contents, partially social and partially individual, but it stands under the fundamental, formative, irreducible category of a unity, which we cannot otherwise express than through the synthesis or the contemporariness of the two logically antithetical determinations—articulation and self-sufficiency, the condition of being produced by, and contained in, society, and on the other hand, of being derived out of and moving around its own center. Society consists not only, as we saw above, of beings that in part are not socialized, but also of others that feel themselves to be, on the one hand, completely social existences, on the other hand, while maintaining the same content, completely individual existences. Moreover these are not two unrelated contiguous standpoints, as if, for instance, one considers the same body now with reference to its weight and now with reference to its color; but the two compose that unity which we call the social being, the synthetic category—as the concept of causation is an aprioristic unity, although it includes the two, in content, quite different elements of the causing and of the effect. That this formation is at our disposal, this ability to derive from beings, each of which may feel itself as the *terminus a quo* and as the *terminus ad quem* of its developments, destinies, qualities, the very concept of society which reckons with those elements, and to recognize the reality corresponding with the concept (Society) as the *terminus a quo* and the *terminus ad quem* of those vitalities and self-determinings—that is an apriori of empirical society, that makes its form possible as we know it.

3. Society is a structure of unlike elements. Even where democratic or socialistic movements plan an "equality," and partially attain it, the thing that is really in question is a like valuation of persons, of perfor-

mances, of positions, while an equality of persons, in composition, in life-contents, and in fortunes cannot come into consideration. And where, on the other hand, an enslaved population constitutes only a mass, as in the great oriental despotisms, this equality of each always concerns only certain sides of existence, say the political or the economic, but never the whole of the same, the transmitted qualities, of which, personal relationships, experiences, not merely within the subjective aspect of life but also on the side of its reactions with other existences, will unavoidably have a certain sort of peculiarity and untransferability. If we posit society as a purely objective scheme, it appears as an ordering of contents and performances which in space, time, concepts, values are concerned with one another, and as to which we may in so far perform an abstraction from the personality, from the Ego-form, which is the vehicle of its dynamic. If that inequality of the elements now presents every performance or equality within this order as individually marked and in its place unequivocally established, at the same time society appears as a cosmos whose manifoldness in being and in movement is boundless, in which, however, each point can be composed and can develop itself only in that particular way, the structure is not to be changed. What has been asserted of the structure of the world in general, viz., that no grain of sand could have another form or place from that which now belongs to it, except upon the presupposition and with the consequence of a change of all being—the same recurs in the case of the structure of society regarded as a web of qualitatively determined phenomena. An analogy as in the case of a miniature, greatly simplified and conventionalized (*stilisiert*), is to be found for the picture of society thus conceived as a whole, in a body of officials, which as such consists of a definite ordering of "positions," of a pre-ordination of performances, which, detached from their personnel of a given moment, present an ideal correlation. Within the same, every newcomer finds an unequivocally assigned place, which has waited for him, as it were, and with which his energies must harmonize. That which in this case is a conscious, systematic assignment of functions, is in the totality of society of course an inextricable tangle of functions; the positions in it are not given by a constructive will, but they are discernible only through the actual doing and experiencing of individuals. And in spite of this enormous difference, in spite of everything that is irrational, imperfect, and from the viewpoint of evaluation to be condemned, in historical society, its phenomenological structure—the sum and the relationship of the sort of existence and performances actually presented by all the elements of objectively historical society is an order of elements, each of which occupies an individually determined place, a coordination of functions and of functioning centers, which are objective and in their social significance full of meaning if not always full of value. At the same time, the purely personal aspect, the subjectively productive, the impulses and reflexes of the essential ego remain entirely out of consideration. Or, otherwise expressed, the life of society runs its course—not psychologically, but phenomenologically, regarded purely with respect to its social contents—as though each element were predetermined for its place in this whole. In the case of every break in the harmony of the ideal demands, it runs as though all the members of this whole stood in a relation of unity, which relation, precisely because each member is his particular self, refers him to all the others and all the others to him.

From this point, then, the apriori is visible which should be now in question, and which signifies to the individual a foundation and a "possibility" of belonging to a society. That each individual, by virtue of his own quality, is automatically referred to a determined position within his social milieu, that this position ideally belonging to him is also actually present in the social whole—this is the presupposition from which, as a basis, the individual leads his societary life, and which we may characterize as the universal value of the individuality. It is independent of the fact that it works itself up toward clear conceptional consciousness, but also of the contingent possibility of finding realization in the actual course of life—as the apriority of the law of causation, as one of the normative preconditions of all cognition, is independent of whether the consciousness formulates it in detached concepts, and whether the psychological reality always proceeds in accordance with it or not. Our cognitive life rests on the presupposition of a pre-established harmony between our spiritual energies, even the most individual of them, and external objective existence, for the latter remains always the expression of the immediate phenomenon, whether or not it can be traced back metaphysically or psychologically to the production of the reality by the intellect itself. Thus societary life as such is posited upon the presupposition of a fundamental harmony between the individual and the social whole, little as this hinders the crass dissonances of the ethical and the eudaemonistic life. If the social reality were unrestrictedly and infallibly given by this preconditional principle, we should have the perfect society—again not in the sense of ethical or eudaemonistic but of conceptual perfection. So far as the individual finds, or does not find, realization of this apriori of his social existence, i.e., the thoroughgoing correlation of his individual being with the surrounding circles, the integrating necessity of his particularity, determined by his subjective personal life, for the life of the whole, the socialization is incomplete; the society has stopped short of being that gapless reciprocality which its concept foretells.

This state of the case comes to a definite focus with the category of the vocation (*Beruf*). Antiquity, to be sure, did not know this concept in the sense of personal differentiation and of the society articulated by division of labor.

But what is at the basis of this conception was in existence even in antiquity; viz., that the socially operative doing is the unified expression of the subjective qualification, that the whole and the permanent of the subjectivity practically objectifies itself by virtue of its functions in the society. This relationship was realized then on the average merely in a less highly differentiated content. Its principle emerged in the Aristotelian dictum that some were destined by their nature to δεσποζειν, others to δουλευειν. With higher development of the concept it shows the peculiar structure—that on the one hand the society begets and offers in itself a position (*Stelle*) which in content and outline differs from others, which, however, in principle may be filled out by many, and thereby is, so to speak, something anonymous; and that this position now, in spite of its character of generality, is grasped by the individual, on the ground of an inner "call," or of a qualification conceived as wholly personal. In order that a "calling" may be given, there must be present, however it came to exist, that harmony between the structure and the life-process of the society on the one side, and the individual make-up and impulses on the other. Upon this as general precondition rests at last the representation that for every personality a position and a function exists within the society, to which the personality is "called," and the imperative to search until it is found.

The empirical society becomes "possible" only through the apriori which culminates in the "vocation" concept, which apriori to be sure, like those previously discussed, cannot be characterized by a simple phrase, as in the case of the Kantian categories. The consciousness processes wherewith socialization takes place—unity composed of many, the reciprocal determination of the individuals, the reciprocal significance of the individual for the totality of the other individuals and of the totality for the individual—run their course under this precondition which is wholly a matter of principle, which is not recognized in the abstract, but expresses itself in the reality of practice: viz., that the individuality of the individual finds a position in the structure of the generality, and still more that this structure in a certain degree, in spite of the incalculability of the individuality, depends antecedently upon it and its function. The causal interdependence which weaves each social element into the being and doing of every other, and thus brings into existence the external network of society, is transformed into a teleological interdependence, so soon as it is considered from the side of its individual bearers, its producers, who feel themselves to be egos, and whose attitude grows out of the soil of the personality which is self-existing and self-determining. That a phenomenal wholeness of such character accommodates itself to the purpose of these individualities which approach it from without, so to speak, that it offers a station for their subjectively determined life-process, at which point the peculiarity of the same becomes a necessary member in the life of the whole—this, as a fundamental category, gives to the consciousness of the individual the form which distinguishes the individual as a social element!

George Herbert Mead

1863-1931

Source: *Journal of Philosophy, Psychology, and Scientific Methods* (1913)
Selection: The Social Self, pp. 374-380

Mead was an American sociologist as well as psychologist and philosopher, who was primarily affiliated with the University of Chicago, where he was one of several distinguished pragmatists. He is generally regarded as one of the founders of the American sociological tradition and considered by many to be the father of the school of "Symbolic Interactionism" in sociology and social psychology. In 1888, Mead graduated from Harvard with a Master's degree in philosophy, where he studied with Josiah Royce, a major influence upon his thought, and William James. He subsequently moved to Leipzig, Germany, to study with psychologist Wilhelm Wundt, and he was also heavily influenced by John Dewey, who led Mead into educational theory. His thinking soon diverged from Dewey's, however, and Mead went on to develop his famous psychological theories of mind, self and society. Throughout his career, Mead published about 100 scholarly articles, reviews, and incidental pieces, but he never published a book. Following his death, several of his students put together and edited four volumes from his lecture notes, numerous unpublished papers, and records of his social psychology course at the University of Chicago. Mead is best known for his work on the nature of the self and intersubjectivity. In the seminal writing below, he describes and analyzes the nature of the "social self."

*

Recognizing that the self can not appear in consciousness as an "I," that it is always an object, *i.e.*, a "me," I wish to suggest an answer to the question, What is involved in the self being an object? The first answer may be that an object involves a subject. Stated in other words, that a "me" is inconceivable without an "I." And to this reply must be made that such an "I" is a presupposition, but never a presentation of conscious experience, for the moment it is presented it has passed into the objective case, presuming, if you like, an "I" that observes—but an "I" that can disclose himself only by ceasing to be the subject for whom the object "me" exists. It is, of course, not the Hegelism of a self that becomes another to himself in which I am interested, but the nature of self as revealed by introspection and subject to our factual analysis. This analysis does reveal, then, in a memory process an attitude of observing oneself in which both the observer and the observed appear. To be concrete, one remembers asking himself how he could undertake to do this, that, or the other, chiding himself for his shortcomings or pluming himself upon his achievements. Thus, in the redintegrated self of the moment passed, one finds both a subject and an object, but it is a subject that is now an object of observation, and has the same nature as the object self whom we present as in intercourse with those about us. In quite the same fashion we remember the questions, admonitions, and approvals addressed to our fellows. But the subject attitude which we instinctively take can be presented only as something experienced—as we can be conscious of our acts only through the sensory processes set up after the act has begun.

The contents of this presented subject, who thus has become an object in being presented, but which still distinguish him as the subject of the passed experience from the "me" whom he addressed, are those images which initiated the conversation and the motor sensations which accompany the expression, plus the organic sensations and the response of the whole system to the activity initiated. In a word, just those contents which go to make up the self which is distinguished from the others whom he addresses. The self appearing as "I" is the memory image self who acted toward himself and is the same self who acts toward other selves.

On the other hand, the stuff that goes to make up the "me" whom the "I" addresses and whom he observes, is the experience which is induced by this action of the "I." If the "I" speaks, the "me" hears. If the "I" strikes, the "me" feels the blow. Here again the "me" consciousness is of the same character as that which arises from the action of the other upon him. That is, it is only as the individual finds himself acting with reference to himself as he acts towards others, that he becomes a subject to himself rather than an object, and only as he is affected by his own social conduct in the manner in which he is affected by that of others, that he becomes an object to his own social conduct.

The differences in our memory presentations of the "I" and the "me" are those of the memory images of the initiated social conduct and those of the sensory responses thereto.

It is needless, in view of the analysis of Baldwin, of Royce and of Cooley and many others, to do more than indicate that these reactions arise earlier in our social conduct with others than in introspective self-consciousness, *i.e.*, that the infant consciously calls the attention of others before he calls his own attention by affecting himself and that he is consciously affected by others before he is conscious of being affected by himself.

The "I" of introspection is the self which enters into social relations with other selves. It is not the "I" that is implied in the fact that one presents himself as a "me. " And the "me" of introspection is the same "me" that is the object of the social conduct of others. One presents himself as acting toward others—in this presentation he is presented in indirect discourse as the subject of the action and is still an object—and the subject of this presentation can never appear immediately in conscious experience. It is the same self who is presented as observing himself, and he affects himself just in so far and only in so far as he can address himself by the means of social stimulation which affect others. The "me" whom he addresses is the "me," therefore, that is similarly affected by the social conduct of those about him.

This statement of the introspective situation, however, seems to overlook a more or less constant feature of our consciousness, and that is that running current of awareness of what we do which is distinguishable from the consciousness of the field of stimulation, whether that field be without or within. It is this "awareness" which has led many to assume that it is the nature of the self to be conscious both of subject and of object—to be subject of action toward an object world and at the same time to be directly conscious of this subject as subject,—"Thinking its nonexistence along with whatever else it thinks." Now, as Professor James pointed out, this consciousness is more logically conceived of as sciousness—the thinker being an implication rather than a content, while the "me" is but a bit of object content within the stream of sciousness. However, this logical statement does not do justice to the findings of consciousness. Besides the actual stimulations and responses and the memory images of these, within which lie perforce the organic sensations and responses which make up the "me," there accompanies a large part of our conscious experience, indeed all that we call self-conscious, an inner response to what we may be doing, saying, or thinking. At the back of our heads we are a large part of the time more or less clearly conscious of our own replies to the remarks made to others, of innervations which would lead to attitudes and gestures answering our gestures and attitudes towards others.

The observer who accompanies all our self-conscious conduct is then not the actual "I" who is responsible for the conduct in *propria persona*—he is rather the response which one makes to his own conduct.

The confusion of this response of ours, following upon our social stimulations of others with the implied subject of our action, is the psychological ground for the assumption that the self can be directly conscious of itself as acting and acted upon. The actual situation is this: The self acts with reference to others and is immediately conscious of the objects about it. In memory it also redintegrates the self acting as well as the others acted upon. But besides these contents, the action with reference to the others calls out responses in the individual himself—there is then another "me" criticizing, approving, and suggesting, and consciously planning, *i.e.*, the reflective self.

It is not to all our conduct toward the objective world that we thus respond. Where we are intensely preoccupied with the objective world, this accompanying awareness disappears. We have to recall the experience to become aware that we have been involved as selves, to produce the self-consciousness which is a constituent part of a large part of our experience. As I have indicated elsewhere, the mechanism for this reply to our own social stimulation of others follows as a natural result from the fact that the very sounds, gestures, especially vocal gestures, which man makes in addressing others, call out or tend to call out responses from himself. He can not hear himself speak without assuming in a measure the attitude which he would have assumed if he had been addressed in the same words by others.

The self which consciously stands over against other selves thus becomes an object, an other to himself, through the very fact that he hears himself talk, and replies. The mechanism of introspection is therefore given in the social attitude which man necessarily assumes toward himself, and the mechanism of thought, in so far as thought uses symbols which are used in social intercourse, is but an inner conversation.

Now it is just this combination of the remembered self which acts and exists over against other selves with the inner response to his action which is essential to the self-conscious ego—the self in the full meaning of the term—although neither phase of self-consciousness, in so far as it appears as an object of our experience, is a subject.

It is also to be noted that this response to the social conduct of the self may be in the role of another—we present his arguments in imagination and do it with his intonations and gestures and even perhaps with his facial expression. In this way we play the roles of all our group; indeed, it is only in so far as we do this that they become part of our social environment—to be aware of another self as a self implies that we have played his role or that of another with whose type we identify him for purposes of intercourse. The inner response to our reaction to others is therefore as varied as is our social environment. Not that we assume the roles of others toward ourselves because we are subject to a mere imitative instinct, but because in responding to ourselves we are in the nature of the case taking the attitude of another than the self that is directly acting, and into this reaction there naturally flows the memory images of the responses of those about us, the memory images of those responses of others which were in answer to like actions. Thus the child can think about his conduct as good or bad only as he reacts to his own acts in the remembered words of his parents. Until this process has been developed into the abstract process of thought, self-consciousness remains dramatic, and the self which is a fusion of the remembered actor and this accompanying chorus is somewhat loosely organized and very clearly social. Later the inner stage changes into the forum and workshop of thought. The features and intonations of the *dramatis personae* fade out and the emphasis falls upon the meaning of the inner speech, the imagery becomes merely the barely necessary cues. But the mechanism remains social, and at any moment the process may become personal.

It is fair to say that the modern western world has lately done much of its thinking in the form of the novel, while earlier the drama was a more effective but equally social mechanism of self-consciousness. And, in passing, I may refer to that need of filling out the bare spokesman of abstract thought, which even the most abstruse thinker feels, in seeking his audience. The import of this for religious self-consciousness is obvious.

There is one further implication of this nature of the self to which I wish to call attention. It is the manner of its reconstruction. I wish especially to refer to it, because the point is of importance in the psychology of ethics.

As a mere organization of habit the self is not self-conscious. It is this self which we refer to as character. When, however, an essential problem appears, there is some disintegration in this organization, and different tendencies appear in reflective thought as different voices in conflict with each other. In a sense the old self has disintegrated, and out of the moral process a new self arises. The specific question I wish to ask is whether the new self appears together with the new object or end. There is of course a reciprocal relation between the self and its object, the one implies the other and the interests and evaluations of the self answer exactly to content and values of the object. On the other hand, the consciousness of the new object, its values and meaning, seems to come earlier to consciousness than the new self that answers to the new object.

The man who has come to realize a new human value is more immediately aware of the new object in his conduct than of himself and his manner of reaction to it. This is due to the fact to which reference has already been made, that direct attention goes first to the object. When the self becomes an object, it appears in memory, and the attitude which it implied has already been taken. In fact, to distract attention from the object to the self implies just that lack of objectivity which we criticize not only in the moral agent, but in the scientist.

Assuming as I do the essentially social character of the ethical end, we find in moral reflection a conflict in which certain values find a spokesman in the old self or a dominant part of the old self, while other values answering to other tendencies and impulses arise in opposition and find other spokesmen to present their cases. To leave the field to the values represented by the old self is exactly what we term selfishness. The justification for the term is found in the habitual character of conduct with reference to these values. Attention is not claimed by the object and shifts to the subjective field where the affective responses are identified with the old self. The result is that we state the other conflicting ends in subjective terms of other selves and the moral problem seems to take on the form of the sacrifice either of the self or of the others.

Where, however, the problem is objectively considered, although the conflict is a social one, it should not resolve itself into a struggle between selves, but into such a reconstruction of the situation that different and enlarged and more adequate personalities may emerge. A tension should be centered on the objective social field.

In the reflective analysis, the old self should enter upon the same terms with the selves whose roles are assumed, and the test of the reconstruction is found in the fact that all the personal interests are adequately recognized in a new social situation. The new self that answers to this new situation can appear in consciousness only after this new situation has been realized and accepted. The new self can not enter into the field as the determining factor because he is consciously present only after the new end has been formulated and accepted. The old self may enter only as an element over against the other personal interests involved. If he is the dominant factor it must be in defiance of the other selves whose interests are at stake. As the old self he is defined by his conflict with the others that assert themselves in his reflective analysis.

Solution is reached by the construction of a new world harmonizing the conflicting interests into which enters the new self.

The process is in its logic identical with the abandonment of the old theory with which the scientist has identified himself, his refusal to grant this old attitude any further weight than may be given to the other conflicting observations and hypotheses. Only when a successful hypothesis, which overcomes the conflicts, has been formulated and accepted, may the scientist again identify himself with this hypothesis as his own, and maintain it *contra mundum*. He may not state the scientific problem and solution in terms of his old personality. He may name his new hypothesis after himself and realize his enlarged scientific personality in its triumph.

The fundamental difference between the scientific and moral solution of a problem lies in the fact that the moral problem deals with concrete personal interests, in which the whole self is reconstructed in its relation to the other selves whose relations are essential to its personality.

The growth of the self arises out of a partial disintegration,—the appearance of the different interests in the forum of reflection, the reconstruction of the social world, and the consequent appearance of the new self that answers to the new object.

William Isaac Thomas

1863-1947

Source: *The Polish Peasant in Europe and America*, Vol. I (with Florian Znaniecki) (1918)
Selection: Methodological Note, pp. 67-87

The American sociologist W. I. Thomas was a full professor at the University of Chicago from 1910 until 1918, when his career was suddenly terminated following charges (which were later dropped) that he violated the Mann Act. Nonetheless he subsequently made major contributions to sociological research and theory, was elected to the presidency of the American Sociological Association in 1926, and is considered one of the founders of "Symbolic Interactionism," along with George Herbert Mead. Many of his seminal concepts are reflected in his major work, The Polish Peasant in Europe and America, *which examined how immigrants adjusted to a new culture. This landmark study, published in five-volumes between 1918 and 1920, with co-author Florian Znaniecki (who originally was Thomas's research assistant), put forward a biographical approach to understanding culture and ethnicity, and also contained a detailed discussion of two seminal concepts—the "situation" and "the definition of the situation." The latter came to be incorporated in what is known as the Thomas theorem: "If men define situations as real they are real in their consequences." The theorem was thus recognized as a link between subjective experience and responsive action, which Thomas applied in various books, such as* The Unadjusted Girl *(1923) and* The Child in America *(1928). Below is the discussion and analysis of the "situation" and the "definition of the situation" in the "Methodological Note" in Volume I of* The Polish Peasant, *along with general commentary about the monographic method and qualitative analysis employed in the landmark study.*

*

Whatever may be the aim of social practice—modification of individual attitudes or of social institutions—in trying to attain this aim we never find the elements which we want to use or to modify isolated and passively waiting for our activity, but always embodied in active practical *situations,* which have been formed independently of us and with which our activity has to comply.

The situation is the set of values and attitudes with which the individual or the group has to deal in a process of activity and with regard to which this activity is planned and its results appreciated. Every concrete activity is the solution of a situation. The situation involves three kinds of data: (1) The objective conditions under which the individual or society has to act, that is, the totality of values—economic, social, religious, intellectual, etc.— which at the given moment affect directly or indirectly the conscious status of the individual or the group. (2) The preexisting attitudes of the individual or the group which at the given moment have an actual influence upon his behavior. (3) The definition of the situation, that is, the more or less clear conception of the conditions and consciousness of the attitudes. And the definition of the situation is a necessary preliminary to any act of the will, for in given conditions and with a given set of attitudes an indefinite plurality of actions is possible, and one definite action can appear only if these conditions are selected, interpreted, and combined in a determined way and if a systematization of these attitudes is reached, so one of them becomes predominant and subordinates the others. It happens, indeed, that a certain value imposes itself immediately and unreflectively and leads at once to action, or that an attitude as soon as it appears excludes the others and expresses itself unhesitatingly in an active process. In these cases, whose most radical examples are found in reflex and instinctive actions, the definition is already given to the individual by external conditions or by his own tendencies. But usually there is a process of reflection, after which either a ready social definition is applied or a new personal defin ition worked out.

Let us take a typical example out of the fifth volume of the present work, concerning the family life of the immigrants in America. A husband, learning of his wife's infidelity, deserts her. The objective conditions were: (1) the social institution of marriage with all the rules involved; (2) the wife, the other man, the children, the neighbors, and in general all the individuals constituting the habitual environment of the husband and, in a sense, given to him as values; (3) certain economic conditions; (4) the fact of the wife's infidelity. Toward all these values the husband had certain attitudes, some of them traditional, others recently developed. Now, perhaps under the influence of the discovery of his wife's infidelity, perhaps after having developed some new attitude toward the sexual or economic side of marriage, perhaps simply influenced by the advice of a friend in the form of a rudimentary scheme of the situation helping him to "see the point," he defines the situation for himself. He takes certain conditions into account, ignores or neglects others, or gives them a certain interpretation in view of some chief value, which may be his wife's infidelity, or the economic burdens of family life of which this infidelity gives him the pretext to rid himself, or perhaps some other woman, or the half-ironical pity of his neighbors, etc. And in this definition some one attitude—sexual jealousy, or desire for economic freedom, or love for the other woman, or offended desire for recognition—or a complex of these attitudes, or a new attitude (hate, disgust) subordinates to itself the others and manifests itself chiefly in the subsequent action, which is evidently a solution of the situation, and fully determined both in its social and in its individual components by the whole set of values, attitudes, and reflective schemes which the situation included. When a situation is solved, the result of the activity becomes an element of a new situation, and this is most clearly evidenced in cases where the activity brings a change of a social institution whose unsatisfactory functioning was the chief element of the first situation.

Now, while the task of science is to analyze by a comparative study the whole process of activity into elementary facts, and it must therefore ignore the variety of concrete situations in order to be able to find laws of causal dependence of abstractly isolated attitudes or values on other attitudes and values, the task of technique is to provide the means of a rational control of concrete situations. The situation can evidently be controlled either by a change of conditions or by a change of attitudes, or by both, and in this respect the role of technique as application of science is easily characterized. By comparing situations of a certain type, the social technician must find what are the predominant values or the predominant attitudes which determine the situation more than others, and then the question is to modify these values or these attitudes in the desired way by using the knowledge of social causation given by social theory. Thus, we may find that some of the situations among the Polish immigrants in America resulting in the husband's desertion are chiefly determined by the wife's infidelity, others by her quarrelsomeness, others by bad economic conditions, still others by the husband's desire for freedom, etc. And, if in a given case we know what influences to apply in order to modify these dominating factors, we can modify the situation accordingly, and ideally we can provoke in the individual a behavior in conformity with any given scheme of attitudes and values.

To be sure, it may happen that, in spite of an adequate scientific knowledge of the social laws permitting the modification of those factors which we want to change, our efforts will fail to influence the situation or will produce a situation more undesirable than the one we wished to avoid. The fault is then with our technical knowledge. That is, either we have failed in determining the relative importance of the various factors, or we have failed to foresee the influence of other causes which, interfering with our activity, produce a quite unexpected and undesired effect. And since it is impossible to expect from every practitioner a complete scientific training and still more impossible to have him work out a scientifically justified and detailed plan of action for every concrete case in particular, the special task of the social technician is to prepare, with the help of both science and practical observation, thorough schemes and plans of action for all the various *types* of situations which may be found in a given line of social activity, and leave to the practitioner the subordination of the given concrete situation to its proper type. This is actually the role which all the organizers of social institutions have played, but the technique must become more conscious and methodically perfect, and every field of social activity should have its professional technicians. The evolution of social life makes necessary continual modifications and developments of social technique, and we can hope the evolution of social theory will continually put new and useful scientific generalizations within the reach of the social technician; the latter must therefore remain in permanent touch with both social life and social theory, and this requires a more far-going specialization than we actually find.

But, however efficient this type of social technique may become, its application will always have certain limits beyond which a different type of technique will be more useful. Indeed, the form of social control outlined above presupposes that the individual—or the group—is treated as a passive object of our activity and that we change the situations for him, from case to case, in accordance with our plans and intentions. But the application of this method becomes more and more difficult as the situations grow more complex, more new and unexpected from case to case, and more influenced by the individual's own reflection. And, indeed, from both the moral and the hedonistic standpoints and also from the standpoint of the level of efficiency of the individual and of the group, it is desirable to develop in the individuals the ability to control spontaneously their own activities by conscious reflection. To use a biological comparison, the type of control where the practitioner prescribes for the individual a scheme of activity appropriate to every crisis as it arises corresponds to the tropic or reflex type of control in animal life, where the activity of the individual is controlled mechanically by stimulations from without, while the reflective and individualistic control corresponds to the type of activity characteristic of the higher conscious organism, where the control is exercised from within by the selective mechanism of the nervous system. While, in the early tribal, communal, kinship, and religious groups, and to a large extent in the historic state, the society itself provided a rigoristic and particularistic set of definitions in the form of "customs" or "mores," the tendency to advance is associated with the liberty of the individual to make his own definitions.

We have assumed throughout this argument that if an adequate technique is developed it is possible to produce any desirable attitudes and values, but this assumption is practically justified only if we find in the individual attitudes which cannot avoid response to the class of stimulations which society is able to apply to him. And apparently we do find this disposition. Every individual has a vast variety of wishes which can be satisfied only by his incorporation in a society. Among his general patterns of wishes we may enumerate: (1) the desire for new experience, for fresh stimulations; (2) the desire for recognition, including, for example, sexual response and general social appreciation, and secured by devices ranging from the display of ornament to the demonstration of worth through scientific attainment; (3) the desire for mastery, or the "will to power," exemplified by ownership, domestic tyranny, political despotism, based on the instinct of hate, but capable of being sublimated to laudable ambition; (4) the desire for security, based on the instinct of fear and exemplified negatively by the wretchedness of the individual in perpetual solitude or under social taboo. Society is, indeed, an agent for the repression of many of the wishes in the individual; it demands that he shall be moral by repressing at least the wishes which are irreconcilable with the welfare of the group, but nevertheless it provides the only medium within which any of his schemes or wishes can be gratified. And it would be superfluous to point out by examples the degree to which society has in the past been able to impose its schemes of attitudes and values on the individual. Professor Sumner's volume, *Folkways,* is practically a collection of such examples, and, far from discouraging us as they discourage Professor Sumner, they should be regarded as proofs of the ability of the individual to conform to any definition, to accept any attitude, provided it is an expression of the public will or represents the appreciation of even a limited group. To take a single example from the present, to be a bastard or the mother of a bastard has been regarded heretofore as anything but desirable, but we have at this moment reports that one of the warring European nations is 'officially impregnating' its unmarried women and girls and even married women whose husbands are at the front. If this is true (which we do not assume) we have a new definition and a new evaluation of motherhood arising from the struggle of this society against death, and we may anticipate a new attitude—that the resulting children and their mothers will be the objects of extraordinary social appreciation. And even if we find that the attitudes are not so tractable as we have assumed, that it is not possible to provoke all the desirable ones, we shall still be in the same situation as, let us say, physics and mechanics: we shall have the problem of securing the highest degree of control possible in view of the nature of our materials.

As to the present work, it evidently cannot in any sense pretend to establish social theory on a definitely scientific basis. It is clear from the preceding discussion that many workers and much time will be needed before we free ourselves from the traditional ways of thinking, develop a completely efficient and exact working method, and reach a system of scientifically correct generalizations. Our present very limited task is the preparation of a certain body of materials, even if we occasionally go beyond it and attempt to reach some generalizations.

Our object-matter is one class of a modern society in the whole concrete complexity of its life. The selection of the Polish peasant society, motivated at first by somewhat incidental reasons, such as the intensity of the Polish immigration and the facility of getting materials concerning the Polish peasant, has proved during the investigation to be a fortunate one. The Polish peasant finds himself now in a period of transition from the old forms of social organization that had been in force, with only insignificant changes, for many centuries, to a modern form of life. He has preserved enough of the old attitudes to make their sociological reconstruction possible, and he is sufficiently advanced upon the new way to make a study of the development of modern attitudes particularly fruitful. He has been invited by the upper classes to collaborate in the construction of Polish national life, and in certain lines his development is due to the conscious educational efforts of his leaders—the nobility, the clergy, the middle class. In this respect he has the value of an experiment in social technique; the successes, as well as the failures, of this educational activity of the upper classes are very significant for social work. These efforts of the upper classes themselves have a particular sociological importance in view of the conditions in which Polish society has lived during the last century. As a society without a state, divided among three states and constantly hampered in all its efforts to preserve and develop a distinct and unique cultural life, it faced a dilemma—either to disappear or to create such substitutes for a state organization as would enable it to resist the destructive action of the oppressing states; or, more generally, to exist without the framework of a state. These substitutes were created, and they are interesting in two respects. First, they show, in an exceptionally intensified and to a large extent isolated form, the action of certain factors of social unity which exist in every society but in normal conditions are subordinated to the state organization and seldom sufficiently accounted for in sociological reflection. Secondly, the lack of permanence of every social institution and the insecurity of every social value in general, resulting from the destructive tendencies of the dominating foreign states, bring with them a necessity of developing and keeping constantly alive all the activities needed to reconstruct again and again every value that had been destroyed. The whole mechanism of social creation is therefore here particularly transparent and easy to understand, and in general the role of human attitudes in social life becomes much more evident than in a society not living under the same strain, but able to rely to a large extent upon the inherited formal organization for the preservation of its culture and unity.

We use in this work the inductive method in a form which gives the least possible place for any arbitrary statements. The basis of the work is concrete materials, and only in the selection of these materials some necessary discrimination has been used. But even here we have tried to proceed in the most cautious way possible. The private letters constituting the first two volumes have needed relatively little selection, particularly as they are arranged in family series. Our task has been limited to the exclusion of such letters from among the whole collection as containing nothing but a repetition of situations and attitudes more completely represented in the materials which we publish here. In later volumes the selection can be more severe, as far as the conclusions of the preceding volumes can be used for guidance.

The analysis of the attitudes and characters given in notes to particular letters and in introductions to particular series contains nothing not essentially contained in the materials themselves; its task is only to isolate single attitudes, to show their analogies and dependences, and to interpret them in relation to the social background upon which they appear. Our acquaintance with the Polish society simply helps us in noting data and relations which would perhaps not be noticed so easily by one not immediately acquainted with the life of the group.

Finally, the synthesis constituting the introductions to particular volumes is also based upon the materials, with a few exceptions where it was thought necessary to draw some data from Polish ethnological publications or systematic studies. The sources are always quoted.

The general character of the work is mainly that of a systematization and classification of attitudes and values prevailing in a concrete group. Every attitude and every value, as we have said above, can be really understood only in connection with the whole social life of which it is an element, and therefore this method is the only one that gives us a full and systematic acquaintance with all the complexity of social life. But it is evident that this monograph must be followed by many others if we want our acquaintance with social reality to be complete. Other Slavic groups, particularly the Russians; the French and the Germans, as representing different types of more efficient societies; the Americans, as the most conspicuous experiment in individualism; the Jews, as representing particular social adaptations under peculiar social pressures; the Oriental, with his widely divergent attitudes and values; the Negro, with his lower cultural level and unique social position—these and other social groups should be included in a series of monographs, which in its totality will give for the first tune a wide and secure basis for any sociological generalizations whatever. Naturally the value of every monograph will increase with the development of the work, for not only will the method continually improve, but every group will help to understand every other.

In selecting the monographic method for the present work and in urging the desirability of the further preparation of large bodies of materials representing the total life of different social groups, we do not ignore the other method of approaching a scientific social theory and practice—the study of special problems, of isolated aspects of social life. And we are not obliged to wait until all the societies have been studied monographically, in their whole concrete reality, before beginning the comparative study of particular problems. Indeed, the study of a single society, as we have undertaken it here, is often enough to show what role is played by a particular class of phenomena in the total life of a group and to give us in this way sufficient indications for the isolation of this class from its social context without omitting any important interaction that may exist between phenomena of this class and others, and we can then use these indications in taking the corresponding kinds of phenomena in other societies as objects of comparative research.

Charles Horton Cooley

1864-1929

Source: *Human Nature and the Social Order* (1902)
Selection: Chapter V: The Social Self—The Meaning of "I," pp. 144-157

Cooley was an American sociologist who initially studied economics, philosophy, and engineering, and worked for two years in Washington for the Interstate Commerce Commission and the Bureau of the Census. His dissertation, entitled "The Theory of Transportation," reflected this background, as it concerned itself with documenting that towns and cities tend to be situated at the convergence of transportation routes. Cooley's interests soon focused on sociological concerns, and he taught sociology at the university of Michigan from 1904-1929. In 1905 he participated in the founding of the American Sociological Society, and in 1918 he served as its eighth President. While he published extensively on various topics during his career, he is best known for his concept of the "looking glass self," which holds that a person's self grows out of society's interpersonal interactions and the perceptions of others. In Human Nature and the Social Order, *published in 1902, where he introduced the theory, Cooley foreshadowed Mead's discussion of the symbolic basis of the self, by describing how social responses affect the emergence of ordinary social participation. Cooley expanded his ideas further in* Social Organization *(1909), where he emphasized the importance of primary groups. The following writing presents his analysis of the meaning of "I" and the "looking glass self."*

*

As many people have the impression that the verifiable self, the object that we name with "I," is usually the material body, it may be well to say that this impression is an illusion, easily dispelled by any one who will undertake a simple examination of facts. It is true that when we philosophize a little about "I" and look around for a tangible object to which to attach it, we soon fix upon the material body as the most available *locus;* but when we use the word naively, as in ordinary speech, it is not very common to think of the body in connection with it; not nearly so common as it is to think of other things. There is no difficulty in testing this statement, since the word "I" is one of the commonest in conversation and literature, so that nothing is more practicable than to study its meaning at any length that may be desired. One need only listen to ordinary speech until the word has occurred, say, a hundred times, noting its connections, or observe its use in a similar number of cases by the characters in a novel. Ordinarily it will be found that in not more than ten cases in a hundred does "I" have reference to the body of the person speaking. It refers chiefly to opinions, purposes, desires, claims, and the like, concerning matters that involve no thought of the body. *I* think or feel so and so; *I* wish or intend so and so; *I* want this or that; are typical uses, the self-feeling being associated with the view, purpose, or object mentioned. It should also be remembered that "my" and "mine" are as much the names of the self as "I," and these, of course, commonly refer to miscellaneous possessions.

I had the curiosity to attempt a rough classification of the first hundred "I's" and "me's" in *Hamlet*, with the following results. The pronoun was used in connection with perception, as "I hear," "I see," fourteen times; with thought, sentiment, intention, etc., thirty-two times; with wish, as "I pray you," six times; as speaking—"I'll speak to it"—sixteen times; as spoken to, twelve times; in connection with action, involving perhaps some vague notion of the body, as "I came to Denmark," nine times; vague or doubtful, ten times; as equivalent to bodily appearance—"No more like my father than I to Hercules"—once. Some of the classifications are arbitrary, and another observer would doubtless get a different result; but he could not fail, I think, to conclude that Shakespeare's characters are seldom thinking of their bodies when they say "I" or "me." And in this respect they appear to be representative of mankind in general.

As already suggested, instinctive self-feeling is doubtless connected in evolution with its important function in stimulating and unifying the special activities of individuals. It appears to be associated chiefly with ideas of the exercise of power, of being a cause, ideas that emphasize the antithesis between the mind and the rest of the world. The first definite thoughts that a child associates with self-feeling are probably those of his earliest endeavors to control visible objects—his limbs, his playthings, his bottle, and the like. Then he attempts to control the actions of the persons about him, and so his circle of power and of self-feeling widens without interruption to the most complex objects of mature ambition. Although he does not say "I" or "my" during the first year or two, yet he expresses so clearly by his actions the feeling that adults associate with these words that we cannot deny him a self even in the first weeks.

The correlation of self-feeling with purposeful activity is easily seen by observing the course of any productive enterprise. If a boy sets about making a boat, and has any success, his interest in the matter waxes, he gloats over it, the keel and stem are dear to his heart, and its ribs are more to him than those of his own frame. He is eager to call in his friends and acquaintances, saying to them, "See what I am doing! Is it not remarkable?" feeling elated when it is praised, and either resentful or humiliated when fault is found with it. But so soon as he finishes it and turns to something else, his self-feeling begins to fade away from it, and in a few weeks at most he will have become comparatively indifferent. We all know that much the same course of feeling accompanies the achievements of adults. It is impossible to produce a picture, a poem, an essay, a difficult bit of masonry, or any other work of art or craft, without having self-feeling regarding it, amounting usually to considerable excitement and desire for some sort of appreciation; but this rapidly diminishes with the activity itself and lapses into indifference after it ceases.

It may perhaps be objected that the sense of self, instead of being limited to times of activity and definite purpose, is often most conspicuous when the mind is unoccupied or undecided, and that the idle and ineffectual are commonly the most sensitive in their self-esteem. This, however, may be regarded as an instance of the principle that all instincts are likely to assume troublesome forms when denied wholesome expression. The need to exert power, when thwarted in the open fields of life, is the more likely to assert itself in trifles.

The social self is simply any idea, or system of ideas, drawn from the communicative life, that the mind cherishes as its own. Self-feeling has its chief scope *within* the general life, not outside of it; the special endeavor or tendency of which it is the emotional aspect finds its principal field of exercise in a world of personal forces, reflected in the mind by a world of personal impressions. As connected with the thought of other persons the self idea is always a consciousness of the peculiar or differentiated aspect of one's life, because that is the aspect that has to be sustained by purpose and endeavor, and its more aggressive forms tend to attach themselves to whatever one finds to be at once congenial to one's own tendencies and at variance with those of others with whom one is in mental contact. It is here that they are most needed to serve their function of stimulating characteristic activity, of fostering those personal variations which the general plan of life seems to require. Heaven, says Shakespeare, doth divide

"The state of man in divers functions,
betting endeavor in continual motion,"

and self-feeling is one of the means by which this diversity is achieved.

Agreeably to this view we find that the aggressive self manifests itself most conspicuously in an appropriativeness of objects of common desire, corresponding to the individual's need of power over such objects to secure his own peculiar development, and to the danger of opposition from others who also need them. And this extends from material objects to lay hold, in the same spirit, of the attentions and affections of other people, of all sorts of plans and ambitions, including the noblest special purposes the mind can entertain, and indeed of any conceivable idea which may come to seem a part of one's life and in need of assertion against some one else. The attempt to limit the word self and its derivatives to the lower aims of personality is quite arbitrary; at variance with common sense as expressed by the emphatic use of "I" in connection with the sense of duty and other high motives, and unphilosophical as ignoring the function of the self as the organ of specialized endeavor of higher as well as lower kinds.

That the "I" of common speech has a meaning which includes some sort of reference to other persons is involved in the very fact that the word and the ideas it stands for are phenomena of language and the communicative life. It is doubtful whether it is possible to use language at all without thinking more or less distinctly of some one else, and certainly the things to which we give names and which have a large place in reflective thought are almost always those which are impressed upon us by our contact with other people. Where there is no communication there can be no nomenclature and no developed thought. What we call "me," "mine," or "myself" is, then, not something separate from the general life, but the most interesting part of it, a part whose interest arises from the very fact that it is both general and individual. That is, we care for it just because it is that phase of the mind that is living and striving in the common life, trying to impress itself upon the minds of others. "I" is a militant social tendency, working to hold and enlarge its place in the general current of tendencies. So far as it can it waxes, as all life does. To think of it as apart from society is a palpable absurdity of which no one could be guilty who really saw it as a fact of life.

"Der Mensch erkennt sich nur im Menschen, nur
Das Leben lehret jedem was er sei." *

(* "Only in man does man know himself; life alone teaches each one what he is." Goethe, Tasso, act 2, sc. 3.)

If a thing has no relation to others of which one is conscious he is unlikely to think of it at all, and if he does think of it he cannot, it seems to me, regard it as emphatically *his*. The appropriative sense is always the shadow, as it were, of the common life, and when we have it we have a sense of the latter in connection with it. Thus, if we think of a secluded part of the woods as "ours," it is because we think, also, that others do not go there. As regards the body I doubt if we have a vivid my-feeling about any part of it which is not thought of, however vaguely, as having some actual or possible reference to some one else. Intense self-consciousness regarding it arises along with instincts or experiences which connect it with the thought of others. Internal organs, like the liver, are not thought of as peculiarly ours unless we are trying to communicate something regarding them, as, for instance, when they are giving us trouble and we are trying to get sympathy.

"I," then, is not all of the mind, but a peculiarly central, vigorous, and well-knit portion of it, not separate from the rest but gradually merging into it, and yet having a certain practical distinctness, so that a man generally shows clearly enough by his language and behavior what his "I" is as distinguished from thoughts he does not appropriate. It may be thought of, as already suggested, under the analogy of a central colored area on a lighted wall. It might also, and perhaps more justly, be compared to the nucleus of a living cell, not altogether separate from the surrounding matter, out of which indeed it is formed, but more active and definitely organized.

The reference to other persons involved in the sense of self may be distinct and particular, as when a boy is ashamed to have his mother catch him at something she has forbidden, or it may be vague and general, as when one is ashamed to do something which only his conscience, expressing his sense of social responsibility, detects and disapproves; but it is always there. There is no sense of "I," as in pride or shame, without its correlative sense of you, or he, or they. Even the miser gloating over his hidden gold can feel the "mine" only as he is aware of the world of men over whom he has secret power; and the case is very similar with all kinds of hid treasure. Many painters, sculptors, and writers have loved to withhold their work from the world, fondling it in seclusion until they were quite done with it; but the delight in this, as in all secrets, depends upon a sense of the value of what is concealed.

In a very large and interesting class of cases the social reference takes the form of a somewhat definite imagination of how one's self—that is any idea he appropriates—appears in a particular mind, and the kind of self-feeling one has is determined by the attitude toward this attributed to that other mind. A social self of this sort might be called the reflected or looking glass self:

> "Each to each a looking-glass
> Reflects the other that doth pass."

As we see our face, figure, and dress in the glass, and are interested in them because they are ours, and pleased or otherwise with them according as they do or do not answer to what we should like them to be; so in imagination we perceive in another's mind some thought of our appearance, manners, aims, deeds, character, friends, and so on, and are variously affected by it.

A self-idea of this sort seems to have three principal elements: the imagination of our appearance to the other person; the imagination of his judgment of that appearance, and some sort of self-feeling, such as pride or mortification. The comparison with a looking-glass hardly suggests the second element, the imagined judgment, which is quite essential. The thing that moves us to pride or shame is not the mere mechanical reflection of ourselves, but an imputed sentiment, the imagined effect of this reflection upon another's mind. This is evident from the fact that the character and freight of that other, in whose mind we see ourselves, makes all the difference with our feeling. We are ashamed to seem evasive in the presence of a straightforward man, cowardly in the presence of a brave one, gross in the eyes of a refined one, and so on. We always imagine, and in imagining share, the judgments of the other mind. A man will boast to one person of an action—say some sharp transaction in trade—which he would be ashamed to own to another.

It should be evident that the ideas that are associated with self-feeling and form the intellectual content of the self cannot be covered by any simple description, as by saying that the body has such a part in it, friends such a part, plans so much, etc., but will vary indefinitely with particular temperaments and environments. The tendency of the self, like every aspect of personality, is expressive of far-reaching hereditary and social factors, and is not to be understood or predicted except in connection with the general life. Although special, it is in no way separate—speciality and separateness are not only different but contradictory, since the former implies connection with a whole. The object of self-feeling is affected by the general course of history, by the particular development of nations, classes, and professions, and other conditions of this sort.

The truth of this is perhaps most decisively shown in the fact that even those ideas that are most generally associated or colored with the "my" feeling, such as one's idea of his visible person, of his name, his family, his intimate friends, his property, and so on, are not universally so associated, but may be separated from the self by peculiar social conditions. Thus the ascetics, who have played so large a part in the history of Christianity and of other religions and philosophies, endeavored not without success to divorce their appropriative thought from all material surroundings, and especially from their physical persons, which they sought to look upon as accidental and degrading circumstances of the soul's earthly sojourn. In thus estranging themselves from their bodies, from property and comfort, from domestic affections—whether of wife or child, mother, brother or sister—and from other common objects of ambition, they certainly gave a singular direction to self-feeling, but they did not destroy it: there can be no doubt that the instinct, which seems imperishable so long as mental vigor endures, found other ideas to which to attach itself; and the strange and uncouth forms which ambition took in those centuries when the solitary, filthy, idle, and sense-tormenting anchorite was a widely accepted ideal of human life, are a matter of instructive study and reflection. Even in the highest exponents of the ascetic ideal, like St. Jerome, it is easy to see that the discipline, far from effacing the self, only concentrated its energy in lofty and unusual channels. The self-idea may be that of some great moral reform, of a religious creed, of the destiny of one's soul after death, or even a cherished conception of the deity. [. . .]

Habit and familiarity are not of themselves sufficient to cause an idea to be appropriated into the self. Many habits and familiar objects that have been forced upon us by circumstances rather than chosen for their congeniality remain external and possibly repulsive to the self; and, on the other hand, a novel but very congenial element in experience, like the idea of a new toy, or, if you please, Romeo's idea of Juliet, is often appropriated almost immediately, and becomes, for the time at least, the very heart of the self. Habit has the same fixing and consolidating action in the growth of the self that it has elsewhere, but is not its distinctive characteristic.

As suggested in the previous chapter, self-feeling may be regarded as in a sense the antithesis, or better perhaps, the complement, of that disinterested and contemplative love that tends to obliterate the sense of a divergent individuality. Love of this sort has no sense of bounds, but is what we feel when we are expanding and assimilating new and indeterminate experience, while self-feeling accompanies the appropriating, delimiting, and defending of a certain part of experience; the one impels us to receive life, the other to individuate it. The self, from this point of view, might be regarded as a sort of citadel of the mind, fortified without and containing selected treasures within, while love is an undivided share in the rest of the universe. In a healthy mind each contributes to the growth of the other: what we love intensely or for a long time we are likely to bring within the citadel, and to assert as part of ourself. On the other hand, it is only on the basis of a substantial self that a person is capable of progressive sympathy or love.

The sickness of either is to lack the support of the other. There is no health in a mind except as it keeps expanding, taking in fresh life, feeling love and enthusiasm; and so long as it does this its self-feeling is likely to be modest and generous; since these sentiments accompany that sense of the large and the superior which love implies. But if love closes, the self contracts and hardens: the mind having nothing else to occupy its attention and give it that change and renewal it requires, busies itself more and more with self-feeling, which takes on narrow and disgusting forms, like avarice, arrogance, and fatuity. It is necessary that we should have self-feeling about a matter during its conception and execution; but when it is accomplished or has failed the self ought to break loose and escape, renewing its skin like the snake, as Thoreau says. No matter what a man does, he is not fully sane or human unless there is a spirit of freedom in him, a soul unconfined by purpose and larger than the practicable world. And this is really what those mean who inculcate the suppression of the self; they mean that its rigidity must be broken up by growth and renewal, that it must be more or less decisively "born again." A healthy self must be both vigorous and plastic, a nucleus of solid, well-knit private purpose and feeling, guided and nourished by sympathy.

Max Weber

1864-1920

Source: *The Protestant Ethic and the Spirit of Capitalism* (1904-05)
Selection: Chapter V: Asceticism and the Spirit of Capitalism, pp. 190-206

The German sociologist, historian, and philosopher Max Weber is regarded as one of the "holy trinity" of sociological theorists, along with Karl Marx and Émile Durkheim. Approaching sociology as a scientific, objective study of social action, Weber insisted that in order to explain and understand social phenomena, it is necessary to take into account people's ideas and the meanings they attribute to events, as well as economic systems, classes, and social structures. In these respects and others, such as the importance Weber attributed to lifestyle and the bureaucratization and rationalization of modern life, his theories often challenge those of Marx. Weber also wrote penetratingly about both methodological issues, such as the use of the "ideal type," and social phenomena he saw as antithetical to the modern world and its underlying process of rationalization, such as charisma and mysticism. Most especially, perhaps, Weber was interested in the interrelationship of religious and economic systems. Among the questions of great importance to him was why capitalism developed in the West, rather than other cultures such as Asia, for example. In The Protestant Ethic and the Spirit of Capitalism, *he proposed the "Protestant ethic" as a pertinent answer. The following section from that classic work, which is also his most controversial, summarizes Weber's thesis and method for arguing the connections between Protestant asceticism and the rise of modern capitalism.*

*

To recapitulate at this point, worldly Protestant asceticism acted powerfully to inhibit people's spontaneous pleasure from possessions; it further constrained their desire to consume in general, especially as regards luxuries. Protestant asceticism, on the other hand, also had the effect of psychologically separating out the attainment of goods from the constraints inherent in traditional ethics. It severed the bonds of the acquisitive impulse by both legalizing it and (in the ways discussed) viewing it as willed by God directly. The crusade to deny bodily temptations and dependence on external things was [. . .] a struggle against irrational use of wealth, not against rational acquisition.

External types of luxury, which were damned as veneration of the flesh, epitomized such irrational use of wealth, according to their creed, even though the feudal mind saw them as natural. On the other hand, their doctrine viewed rational and utilitarian uses of wealth with approval, as if God willed them to satisfy both individual and communal needs. Their intention was not to shame wealthy men, but, rather, to focus on how they used their wealth for things, both necessary and useful. The amount of expenditures ethically permissible is constrained by the idea of comfort. Naturally, it is not an accident that the evolution of a way of living harmoniously with that idea can initially be seen most clearly among the most reliable representatives of that entire attitude toward life. Beyond the sparkle and flamboyance of feudal splendor, which rested on a flawed economic foundation and favored squalid elegance over austere simplicity, they held their ideal to be the pristine and solidly comfortable middle-class home.

Asceticism promoted the production of private wealth by condemning dishonesty and reckless greed. Pursuing riches for their own sake was a temptation damned as greediness, Mammonism, etc. In this respect, however, asceticism was a power "which forever seeks good but forever creates evil;" the evil, according to its doctrine, was the temptation of possession. As such, asceticsm conformed to the Old Testament and corresponded to the ethical judgment of good works, because it viewed as highly reprehensible seeking wealth as an end in itself; attaining wealth, however, as a fruit of labor from a calling signaled God's blessing. Even more important: the great religious value placed on ceaseless, continuous, methodical work in the service of a worldly calling as the ultimate path to asceticism, and, simultaneously, as the most certain and obvious proof of renewal and genuine faith, was certainly the most powerful force imaginable to spur on the attitude toward life that has been identified herein as the spirit of capitalism.

When a newfound burst of acquisitive activity is combined with a halter on consumption, the obvious, inevitable, practical result is the accumulation of capital through the ascetic impulse to save. Wealth increased, of course, because of the fetters imposed on the consumption of wealth, which made the productive investment of capital possible. One cannot, unfortunately, state the strength of such influence through statistical means. This connection is so clearly evident in New England that Doyle, a perceptive historian, could not fail to take note of it. In Holland, too, although dominated by a stringent Calvinism for only seven years, the combination of both great wealth and simplicity of life among the most serious religious groups led to an extreme tendency towards accumulation.

It is also evident that the tendency that has existed universally, at all times, and is now very strong in Germany, for the nobility to absorb the fortunes of the middle-class, was unavoidably halted by the Puritan aversion to the feudal way of life. In the seventeenth century, English Mercantilist writers credited the superiority of Dutch over English capital to the fact that those who recently acquired wealth there did not regularly seek to invest in land. In addition, since more is involved than merely a question of purchasing land, there was a failure to seek to adopt feudal habits of life, and thus to eliminate the opportunity for capitalistic investment. [. . .] Since the seventeenth century, throughout all of English society, there has existed the conflict between the squirearchy, who represent "Merrie Old England," and the Puritan assemblages who differ greatly in their social influence. Even today, the characteristics that these societal elements represent, that of a simple, unspoiled joy of life and that of a highly reserved, regulated, self-controlled, and traditional ethical conduct, combine to form the national character of the English. The initial history of the North American colonies was similarly dominated by the striking contrast between the adventurers, who wanted to establish plantations and live as feudal lords, with indentured servants providing the labor, and the Puritans, with their distinctively middle-class outlook.

Wherever the influential Puritan viewpoint existed, in every circumstance—and this is much more important, of course, than simply fostering capital accumulation—it encouraged a rational, bourgeois economic life to develop; this viewpoint was the most important and, even more, it was the only unswerving influence in the development of that life. It took root in the heart of modern economic man.

These Puritanical ideals tended to buckle, of course, when subjected to extreme pressures from the temptations of wealth, which the Puritans knew very well. We regularly find those most authentically dedicated to Puritanism among the classes ascending from a lowly status, the small bourgeois and farmers, while the *beati possidentes*, even among Quakers, frequently tend to renounce their old ideals. The same fate repeatedly befell the monastic asceticism of the Middle Ages, which was the forerunner of the Puritan worldly asceticism. In the former case, when the full effects of rational economic activity had unfolded, from the stringent regulation of conduct and curb on consumption, the wealth that was accumulated either yielded directly to the nobility, as before the Reformation, or there was the threat of a breakdown of monastic authority, which necessary resulted in one of the many reformations.

The entire history of monasticism is actually the history of an ongoing struggle with the problem of wealth and its secularizing influence, viewed a certain way. This is also true, when considered broadly, for the worldly asceticism of Puritanism. Such monastic reform can be compared with the great resurgence of Methodism that preceded the growth of industry in England near the end of the eighteenth century. At this point we present the following quotation from John Wesley, which can effectively serve as a maxim for what has been said above. It illustrates that the leaders of the ascetic movements understood the apparently paradoxical relationships, analyzed above in detail, and that we have given them. He wrote:

> I fear, wherever riches have increased, the essence of religion has decreased in the same proportion. Therefore I do not see how it is possible, in the nature of things, for any revival of true religion to continue long. For religion must necessarily produce both industry and frugality. And these cannot but produce riches. But as riches increase, so will pride, anger, and love of the world in all its branches.
>
> How then is it possible that Methodism, that is, the religion of the heart, though it flourishes now as a green bay-tree, should continue in this state? For the Methodists in every place grow diligent and frugal: consequently they increase in goods. Hence they proportionably increase in pride, in anger, in the desire of the flesh, the desire of the eyes, and the pride of life. So, although the form of religion remains, the spirit is swiftly vanishing away.
>
> Is there no way to prevent this? This continual declension of pure religion? We ought not to forbid people to be diligent and frugal: *we must exhort all Christians to gain all they can, and to save all they can: that is, in-effect, to grow rich!*

Following the above, Wesley advices that those who gain and save all they possibly can also should give all they can, so that their grace increases and they store up wealth in heaven. In his writings, Wesley clearly expresses in detail exactly what we have been trying to emphasize. As he says, the full economic impact of the great ascetic religious movements, which were ultimately important for economic growth and, above all, derived from their educative influence, primarily came after the purely religious fervor had peaked. Only then did the passion of the search for the Kingdom of God start to steadily transform into abstemious economic virtue; the roots of religion gradually died, and gave way to a worldliness marked by utilitarianism. Then, as Dowden said, with reference to Robinson Crusoe, the economic man who is isolated and incidentally carries out missionary activities replaces the forlorn spiritual search of Bunyan's pilgrim for the Kingdom of Heaven, racing around the marketplace of Vanity. Later, as Dowden remarked, when the principle "to make the best of both worlds" became dominant, in the end, a good conscience merely became one of the ways to enjoy a bourgeois life of comfort, as expressed clearly in the German proverb about the soft pillow. However, the great religious era of the seventeenth century gave to its utilitarian successor, more than anything else, an incredibly good, we can even say an excessively pious good, conscience regarding acquiring money, so long as it occurred through legal practices. All traces of the *deplacere vix potest* had disappeared.

A mature, distinctively bourgeois economic ethic had emerged. The bourgeois business man who stayed within the boundaries of what was formally correct, whose moral conduct was flawless, and who put his wealth to uses that were not offensive, could pursue his economic interests and feel he was fulfilling a duty in so doing, all with the consciousness that he was standing in the richness of God's grace and was evidently being blessed by Him. Furthermore, the power of religious asceticism gave the business man highly industrious workmen who were restrained, conscientious, and dedicated to their work, as if it were a life mission that was willed by God.

Finally, the business man was soothed by the promise that the unequal distribution of worldly goods was a special consideration of Divine Providence, and thus such differences, as in scrupulous grace, followed ends that were secret and unknown to men. Calvin made the oft-quoted statement that it was only when people were poor, i. e., the mass of laborers and craftsmen, that they remained subservient to God. In the Netherlands (Pieter de la Court and others), that doctrine had been secularized to mean that the majority of men labor only when forced by necessity to do so. This conception was a leading idea of capitalistic economy and subsequently became part of current theories about the effect of low wages on productivity. Here, also, following the developmental progression that we have observed repeatedly, the extinction of the religious root allowed the utilitarian interpretation to sneak in unseen.

Medieval ethics did much more than merely tolerate begging, it truly glorified it in the mendicant orders. Even beggars who were non-religious were at times considered and treated as an estate, since they afforded the person of means a chance to do good works by giving alms. Even the Stuarts, with their Anglican social ethic, closely embraced this attitude. This situation fundamentally changed when Puritan asceticism participated in the harsh English Poor Relief Legislation. That was possible to do since both the Protestant sects and austere Puritan communities were unaware of any begging taking place in their midst.

This may be contrasted to the situation when viewed from the side of the worker. The Zinzendorf branch of Pietism, for example, glorified the loyal worker who rejected the acquisitive impulse, but, instead lived in accordance with the apostolic model, and, therefore, was empowered with the *charisma* of the disciples. The Baptists once prevalently held similar ideas.

Of course the entire ascetic literature, of virtually every denomination, is replete with the idea that dedicated labor is extremely pleasing to God, even when it is done for low wages, performed by those lacking other opportunities in life. As such, nothing new was added by Protestant asceticism itself. It very powerfully deepened this idea, however, and also created the crucial force that allowed it to be effective: the psychological approval of it by conceiving of such labor as a calling, as the ultimate, and often, in the final analysis, the sole means of achieving the certainty of grace. It also legalized, on the other hand, the exploitation of this intense motivation to work, because it simultaneously interpreted the employer's business activity as a calling. It is evident how the doctrine of fulfilling one's duty in the calling as the ultimate way to search for the Kingdom of God, combined with the harsh asceticism that Church discipline naturally imposed, especially on propertyless classes, was certain to affect the productivity of labor, in the capitalistic sense of that term. Viewing labor as a calling defined the modern worker in a manner corresponding to the attitude of viewing the business man in terms of acquisition. Seeing this situation, which was new at the time, caused Sir William Petty, an able observer, as to attribute Holland's economic power in the seventeenth century to the fact that the great number of dissidents there (Calvinists and Baptists) "are thinking, sober men, for the most part, and thus believe their duty towards God is Labour and Industry." [. . .]

This analysis has sought to show that a fundamental element of the spirit of modern capitalism, and of all modern culture—rational conduct based on the idea of the calling—was born from the spirit of Christian asceticism. One need only reread the quotation from Franklin near the beginning of this text to see that the fundamental elements of the attitude, therein called the spirit of capitalism, are identical to what we have just shown to constitute the content of Puritan worldly asceticism, albeit without the religious foundation that had disappeared by Franklin's time. The notion that an ascetic attitude characterizes modern labor is, to be sure, not new. A condition of all valuable work in the modern world is that it is limited by specialization, and includes the renunciation of the Faustian universality of man; today, therefore, conduct and renunciation unavoidably condition each other. This basic, ascetic trait of middle-class life, to the extent it endeavors to be a way of life at all rather than its direct opposite, is what Goethe, at the peak of his wisdom, sought to teach in the *Wanderjahren*, and is ultimately what he bestowed on the life of his *Faust*. For him this insight represented a renunciation, a removal from a time when humanity was complete and beautiful, which cannot be repeated during the course of our cultural progression any more than can the blossoming of ancient Athenian culture.

The Puritan was motivated to labor in a calling, but we do so as if forced. Because when asceticism started to dictate worldly morality, as it disseminated from monastic enclaves into the daily life of society, it helped to create the vast cosmos of the current economic system. This system is tied to the conditions of machine production, both technical and economic, that now determines with irresistible force the lives of everyone born into this structure, not just those directly involved with economic acquisition. This system may, perhaps, determine their lives until the last ton of fossilized coal is burned. According to Baxter, concern for external goods should rest only on the shoulders of the "saint like a light cloak that can be cast aside at any moment." Fate declared, however, that the cloak should transform into an iron cage.

Since the goal of asceticism was to redesign the world and express its ideals in the world, the power of material goods over the lives of men is greater now than at any other time in history, and relentlessly increasing. The spirit of religious asceticism today has escaped from the cage—whether finally, who can say? Its support is no longer needed by triumphant capitalism, however, since it rests on mechanical foundations. The rosy glow of the Enlightenment, its smiling successor, also appears to be vanishing permanently, and the notion of having an obligation to one's calling is like the ghost of dead religious beliefs that haunt our lives. When the individual cannot directly relate the main spiritual and cultural values to the realization of the calling, or on the other hand, simply not feel it to be an economic compulsion, then the individual usually abandons all effort to justify it. In the United States, where it is most highly developed, the pursuit of riches is without religious and ethical meaning, and thus is inclined to be related to purely mundane passions, which gives it the quality of sport in many instances.

In the future no one knows who will live in this cage, or if totally new prophets will arise at the end of this vast expansion or there will be a great revival of old ideas and ideals, or, if neither of these, then mechanized fossilization, inflated with a kind of spasmodic self-importance. Because it can truly be said about the final stage of this cultural development: "Specialists without spirit, sensualists without heart; this void imagines it has reached a level of civilization never previously achieved."

This, then, takes us to the sphere of judgments about value and faith, which need not encumber this exclusively historical discussion. Instead, the next step would be to demonstrate the importance of ascetic rationalism, which we have only alluded to in the foregoing discussion, for the substance of practical social ethics and, therefore, for the kinds of organizations and functions of social groups, from the secret assembly to the state. Then we would have to analyze its connections to humanistic rationalism, its ideals of life and cultural influence; also to the development of philosophical and scientific empiricism, technical development, and spiritual ideals. Then we would have to map out, for every aspect of ascetic religion, its historical development from the medieval origins of worldly asceticism to its passing into pure utilitarianism. Only in this way could we estimate the measurable cultural importance of ascetic Protestantism in relation to the other synthetic elements of modern culture.

We have tried here only to map out the fact and direction of its influence to their motives in one, though a very important, point. It would also be necessary, however, to examine how the totality of social conditions in turn, especially economic, influenced the development and character of Protestant Asceticism. Modern man, even with the best of intention, is generally unable to convey the significance of religious ideas for culture and national character, which they merit. It is, however, not my purpose, of course, to replace a biased materialistic with an equally biased spiritualistic causal interpretation of culture and history. Each one is equally possible, but if each does not serve as the preparation rather than as the conclusion of an investigation, then each will accomplish the same small amount in the service of historical truth.

Works Cited

Comte, A. (1858 [1830-42]). *The Positive Philosophy of Auguste Comte, Freely Translated and Condensed by Harriet Martineau.* New York: Calvin Blanchard.

Cooley, C. H. (1902). *Human Nature and the Social Order*. New York: Scribner's.

Durkheim, É. (1912 [1895]). *Le Règles de la Méthode Sociologique, Sixième Édition (The Rules of Sociological Method, Sixth Edition).* Paris: Librairie Alcan. [Pages 5-19 trans. ©Gordian Knot Books 2010]

Giddings, F. H. (1901). *Inductive Sociology, A Syllabus of Methods, Analyses and Classifications, and Provisionally Formulated Laws.* New York: The Macmillan Company.

Le Bon, G. (1896 [1895]). *The Crowd: A Study of the Popular Mind.* Transl. not given. New York: The Macmillan Company.

Marx, K. & Engels, F. (1906 [1848]). *The Manifesto of the Communist Party.* Authorized English Translation: Edited and Annotated by Frederick Engels, Trans. by Samuel Moore. Chicago: Charles H. Kerr & Company.

Mead, G. H. (1913). "The Social Self," *Journal of Philosophy, Psychology, and Scientific Methods, 10*, pp. 374- 380.

Simmel, G. (1910-11). "How is Society Possible?" *American Journal of Sociology vol. 16*, pp. 372-391.

Spencer, H. (1906 [1873]). *The Study of Sociology.* New York: D. Appleton & Company.

Sumner, W. G. (1906). *Folkways: A Study of the Sociological Importance of Usages, Manners, Customs, Mores, and Morals.* Boston, MA: Ginn and Company.

Tarde, G. (1903 [1890]). *The Laws of Imitation*, Transl. E. C. Parsons. New York: Henry Holt & Co.

Thomas, W. I. & Znaniecki, F. (1918). *The Polish Peasant in Europe and America, Vol. I.* Boston, MA: Richard G. Badger/The Gorham Press.

Tönnies, F. (1920 [1887]). *Gemeinschaft und Gesellschaft*. Berlin: Karl Curtius. [Pages 199-204 trans. © Gordian Knot Books 2010]

Veblen, T. (1918 [1899]). *The Theory of the Leisure Class: An Economic Study of Institutions.* New York: B. W. Huebsch.

Ward, L. F. (1906). *Applied Sociology: A Treatise on the Conscious Improvement of Society by Society,* New York: Ginn and Company.

Weber, M. (1904-05). *Die protestantische Ethik und der Geist des Kapitalismus (The Protestant Ethic and the Spirit of Capitalism.)* From: http://www.zeno.org/Soziologie/M/Weber,+Max/Schriften+zur+Religionssoziologie/Die+protestantische+Ethik+und+der+Geist+des+Kapitalismus. [Pages 190-206 trans. © Gordian Knot Books 2010]

Additional Recommended Books and Websites

Many print and electronic sources are devoted to the founders of sociology and their writings. Below are a few to help you further explore this area of study. Some of these sources contain extensive bibliographies, and the websites have links to other sites you will find of great value.

Books

Aron, R. (1998 ed.). *Main Currents in Sociological Thought.* Piscataway, NJ: Transaction Publishers.

Calhoun, C. (Ed.). (2007). *Sociology in America: A History.* Chicago: University of Chicago Press.

Halsey, A. H. (2004). *A History of Sociology in Britain: Science, Literature, and Society.* Oxford: Oxford University Press.

Lengermann, P. M. & Niebrugge-Brantley, J. (Eds.). (1997). *The Women Founders: Sociology and Social Theory, 1830-1930: A Text/Reader.* Boston: McGraw-Hill.

Martindale, D. (1960). *The Nature and Types of Sociological Theory. Boston: Houghton Mifflin Company.*

Mead, G. H. (1962). *Mind, Self, and Society.* Chicago: University of Chicago Press.

Nisbet, R. A. (1966). *The Sociological Tradition.* London: Heinemann.

Ritzer, G. (Ed.). (2007). *The Blackwell Encyclopedia of Sociology.* Hoboken, NJ: Wiley-Blackwell

Ritzer, George. (2007). *Classical Sociological Theory, 5th Edition.* NY: McGraw-Hill.

Small, A. (1924). *Origins of Sociology.* Chicago: University of Chicago Press.

Weber, M. (1998). *The Protestant Ethic and the Spirit of Capitalism.* Transl. by T. Parsons. Los Angeles: Roxbury Publishing Company, Second Edition.

Websites

Blackwell Encyclopedia of Sociology Online.
http://www.sociologyencyclopedia.com/public/

August Comte and Positivism.
http://membres.multimania.fr/clotilde/

Dead Sociologists Society.
http://media.pfeiffer.edu/lridener/DSS/DEADSOC.HTML
Émile Durkheim Archive.
http://durkheim.itgo.com/main.html
George's Pages, the Mead Project Website.
http://www.brocku.ca/MeadProject/
History of Sociology Section of the American Sociological Association.
http://www.mtholyoke.edu/courses/etownsle/HOS/
Les Classiques des science sociale.
http://classiques.uqac.ca/index.html
Marx & Engels Internet Archive.
http://www.marxists.org/archive/marx/
Sociosite: Famous Sociologists.
http://www.sociosite.net/topics/sociologists.php
Theory Section of the American Sociological Association.
http://www.asatheory.org/
Thorstein Veblen.
http://socserv.socsci.mcmaster.ca/~econ/ugcm/3ll3/veblen/
Verstehen: The Sociology of Max Weber.
http://www.faculty.rsu.edu/~felwell/Theorists/Weber/Whome.htm
WWW Virtual Library: Sociology: Sociological Theory and Theorists.
http://socserv.mcmaster.ca/w3virtsoclib/theories.htm

CPSIA information can be obtained at www.ICGtesting.com
Printed in the USA
266820BV00002B/4/P

9 781884 092978